NONDUAL
LOVE

NONDUAL LOVE

AWAKENING TO THE
LOVING NATURE OF REALITY

· · · · ·

A. H. Almaas

FOREWORD BY RAM DASS

SHAMBHALA

Shambhala Publications, Inc.
2129 13th Street
Boulder, Colorado 80302
www.shambhala.com

Cover design: Katrina Noble
Interior design: Kate Huber-Parker

9 8 7 6 5 4 3 2 1

First Edition
Printed in the United States of America

Shambhala Publications makes every effort
to print on acid-free, recycled paper.

Shambhala Publications is distributed worldwide by
Penguin Random House, Inc., and its subsidiaries.

LIBRARY OF CONGRESS CATALOGING-IN-PUBLICATION DATA
Names: Almaas, A. H., author.
Title: Nondual love: awakening to the loving nature of reality / A. H.
    Almaas; foreword by Ram Dass.
Description: First edition. | Boulder, Colorado: Shambhala, [2023] |
    Includes index.
Identifiers: LCCN 2022019747 | ISBN 9781645471516 (acid-free paper)
Subjects: LCSH: Love—Religious aspects. | Spirituality. | Reality.
Classification: LCC BL325.L67 A46 2023 | DDC 204/.4—dc23/eng20220722
LC record available at https://lccn.loc.gov/2022019747

In loving memory—

This book of human goodness is dedicated
to my friend of many decades,
Hameed Qabazard.
Hameed was a true human being,
whose love flowed toward all,
generous and unhindered.
Over the years, he contributed to the
cover art of many of my books.
His presence in work and play, in friendship and family,
was enjoyed by many as he enjoyed life
the way a human being can.

CONTENTS

Series Foreword

The three books in the Journey of Spiritual Love series by A. H. Almaas offer an excellent road map for bringing you to inner love . . . spiritual love.

When I met my guru, Neem Karoli Baba, my perception of myself—and the universe—changed. He mirrored my soul back to me. Prior to that, I had known my soul, but my guru helped me to shift my perception in order to see that the soul, itself, is love.

Now I love everyone and everything. Being love is a matter of perception. The trees, the clouds, and everything are all made up of love. I love the floor and the ceiling . . . which are also made of love. I even work on loving the souls of difficult people. The only thing that has to shift for us to see love in everything and everyone is our perception.

The soul is love, wisdom, compassion, peace, and joy. I drop inward to move from the mind down into the spiritual heart. The spiritual heart is the doorway to the next plane of consciousness . . . "soul land."

May these books offer a blessing to you as you make that journey—from the mind into the soul . . .

The journey home.

With Love, Ram Dass
Maui, Hawaii
August 2019

Editor's Preface

Have you ever found yourself in a situation where a sweetness arising in your heart catches you by surprise? In this form of heart awakening I am thinking of, the felt sense is strong enough to loosen the grip of the mind and its persistent train of thought. A warm glow expands in your chest as your heart opens. Your consciousness seems to relax and soften. There is a profound shift in how you view the world and yourself. Edges become less pronounced, a smile creeps onto your face, and a palpable goodness seems to permeate you and your surroundings. Perhaps this happens as your attention is focused on the loveliness of a particular person or object, but you soon become aware that the experience encompasses much more. You become aware of the loveliness of everyone and everything. The whole world seems to emanate a pervasive, gentle sweetness that eases your heart and calms your mind. Life at that moment feels good, regardless of what is happening. Where you are is the right place to be and you feel at one with the amazing richness of life unfolding. All is well.

These tend to be fleeting moments, which seem to reflect some kind of magical transformation of reality into a warm and welcoming, sweet and tender world. A world where we feel held, where we can relax without worry, and where we can be the essence of who we are in an easy way. This book invites us into a deep exploration of what is happening to our consciousness when this transformation occurs. What has taken place to bring about this shift in the way things appear and how we experience our own state of being? What does such an experience tell us about reality itself and our place in it? And how does this relate to whatever notion we have of divinity and its loving nature?

In spiritual realms, this has been referred to as universal love, Christ consciousness, or divine bliss. It is a state in which we become aware that we are not separate from the rest of reality, that this reality is permeated by a fundamental goodness and sweetness, and that we no longer feel contained and isolated within the boundaries of our body. We are brought into a direct experience of what is called the nondual world, where there is no subject and object polarity, no separating boundaries of any kind, and no sense that our consciousness has limits. We feel part of a oneness that includes all of reality and from which we cannot be separated.

Nondual Love is an introduction to this state of consciousness, which Almaas calls Divine Love. He shows us that it is one of the true ways that reality appears and one that is available to all of us. For most of us, this boundless love is an accidental occurrence, an act of grace that we have no control over. And indeed, Almaas confirms that it is not possible to control when it appears in our consciousness. He does, however, bring a great deal of understanding and experience to what stops divine love from arising. As well as describing the many ways we can experience and recognize this expansive loving ground of being, perhaps even more importantly he shows us the particular beliefs and positions we tend to identify with that block this experience of oneness. In particular, he speaks of the deep attachments we develop to what we believe we are separate from—the positive attachment to people and things we seek to acquire and hold on to and the negative attachment to what we seek to reject and eliminate. He also speaks of the primitive fears and the defensive posture in our soul that they generate, and how that causes us to deny the reality of something greater and lose sight of the benevolent and beautiful nature of that reality.

This book is a compelling companion volume to *Love Unveiled*, in which Almaas describes the way spiritual love arises within a more familiar world of duality and separateness. Following that love leads us deeper in our hearts and souls, inviting a permeability in us to the mystery of who and what we are. *Nondual Love* picks up where *Love Unveiled* leaves off, by opening up the question of what it means to go beyond the dimension of the individual soul. It follows the thread of longing in the heart to know oneness and unity and no longer be trapped in our separate identities and divided consciousness. After all, deep in our souls is a knowing that our beingness and existence is not separate from the beingness of everything and all of existence.

As always, the power of Almaas's approach is in its focus on one's actual experience, not just the ideas and articulations of the spiritual realm—here the divine consciousness. This orientation is central to the Diamond Approach™, a path of inner realization that he founded and teaches through the Ridhwan School. In this book, which is based on his teaching to members of the School, he constantly invites us into the felt sense of what is real in us, including the taste and feel of this divine love. Supporting this focus are the exercises included in each chapter, which provide an opportunity to explore what he is offering as he expands our perspective on reality and the world we live in.

I welcome you on this journey with him as it knocks on the doors of our tender and loving hearts, asking us to awaken to so much more that is possible in who and what we are. This particular dimension of reality—the fundamental goodness that underlies all manifestation—is sorely missing in most contemporary discourse, relating, and functioning. An awareness of it inevitably shifts our priorities as it softens our boundaries, opens our eyes, and tenderizes our hearts. We all will benefit from knowing directly in our souls the loving nature of being—nondual love—the sweet source of the universe within each of us.

BYRON BROWN

ACKNOWLEDGMENTS

The teaching which forms the basis of this book was presented to members of the Ridhwan School in 1995. I would like to thank those students that provided their time and skill for transcribing the recordings of this material.

We are finally bringing this teaching to the public as part of this three-volume series on spiritual love. Twenty-five years after the original teaching, Paul Hancock took on the task of preparing the text for publication. In his desire to be true to my teaching, he began by reviewing all of the original recordings to clarify places in the transcript that were indicated as "inaudible" or were simply inaccurate based on a closer listening. This also gave him a firsthand encounter with the divine love teaching, as he was not in the School when this was taught many years ago. In addition, Paul had a steep learning curve to take on his first full book of my work, but he has shown himself up to the task. He has brought a combination of a passionate love of this material, a creativity and skill with words, and a strong desire to make my words accessible to a wide audience. I feel great appreciation for Paul's contribution to the creation of this second volume in the Journey of Spiritual Love series.

The creation of this book has also brought about a good working alliance between Paul and my chief editor, Byron Brown, and I am most appreciative of this. Their work together has been essential for transforming the original transcripts into an effective experience of spiritual exploration and transmission for the reader. Byron continues to steer the ship of book development with clarity and care as he brings together the editing, my involvement, and the communication and interaction with Shambhala around review, titling, and cover creation. I feel grateful to him and the wisdom he has developed as publishing director for my books over these many years.

Once again, I want to thank Liz Shaw, my contact and editor at Shambhala Publications, for her care and attention to what it is I am wanting to pass on in this and all my books. Her dedication and consistency of support for my vision has been invaluable. I also thank Audra Figgins for her attention to the layout and final details of presenting the book in a beautiful form.

INTRODUCTION

This book is the second volume in a trilogy of books on love, in which I aim to present the immediate experience of love on the spiritual path. It is the essence of love that we are concerned with here, love that is a pure expression of our spiritual nature, and I look at the many different ways it can be experienced, from the most easily accessible to the deepest and most difficult.

The first volume, *Love Unveiled*, introduces this pure spiritual love in the forms that are more easily recognized by most human beings. These are the essential prototypes of the kinds of love human beings experience on the emotional level, and they are introduced as qualities of pure consciousness, as different ways that spiritual presence manifests. These forms of spiritual or essential love do not require full spiritual awakening or ego death, and hence they are helpful and useful both in everyday life and in traversing the spiritual path to realization and liberation.

This second volume introduces what I term "divine love." This is universal or nondual love, when our spiritual nature manifests its unbounded infinity as a shoreless ocean of sweetness, softness, and goodness. I explore three different ways this nondual love can be experienced: as an ocean of love that we become aware of as it impacts our perception of the physical world; as our own be-ingness felt as a boundless expanse of presence that is pleasurable, generous, and sweet—the unity of reality as love; and as a benevolent vastness that personally loves all the particulars of the world. I refer to the last two ways of experiencing it as realization, for in them, we know ourselves as this expanse of love. Or we could say more precisely that the loving expanse experiences and knows itself simply by being itself, which at the same time is our being.

This book also explores what obstructs access to this boundless dimension of our true nature. It investigates in detail how the belief in being a separate self functions as the main obstacle. But I also consider other obstacles, beliefs, and types of conditioning that stand in the way of true nature manifesting itself as this expanse of pure selfless love.

It is important as we delve into the loving ground of being to understand how this universal love relates to our sense of being an individual consciousness, how it relates to all forms of the world, both inner and outer, and how it relates to our true nature. We see in this process that boundless love is a primary way of knowing and experiencing nondual reality. This is where the expanse of love is inseparable from everything—it is in fact arising as the nature of everything—and shows that divine love is the basis of the universe, of all manifestation and experience.

I differ from those nondual teachings that maintain the spiritual expanse is always manifest but we are simply not aware of it. I prefer the view that the spiritual expanse, and all spiritual potential, only manifests when we are ready for it and open to it. This changes how we look at life and the ordinary world and its relation to the spiritual expanse, in this case, to boundless love. Our familiar world is not simply a delusion or a wrong version of reality but a true way that reality manifests that can be enhanced or transformed through a journey of revelation.

This perspective leads to ways of experiencing the loving non-dual ground of being that make it easier to understand how we can live it and not simply be it. This book demonstrates clearly how this loving dimension of our true nature is the essence of generosity, selfless giving, and service. It is also the realm of beauty, grace, and fundamental goodness. As we recognize the nature of this love dimension, it becomes clear that it is the essence of heart and the origin of all our feelings. For love is the original primordial feeling.

The first two volumes of this Journey of Spiritual Love series prepare us for the third volume, which covers the journey of the heart toward the realization of the Absolute dimension of spiritual nature. There are many ways of realizing ourselves as this absolute mystery that is beyond being and nonbeing, and in the third book I explore one of those ways—the way of the heart. I use my own heart's journey and mystical poetry to illustrate how love is inherently a movement toward the true beloved of the heart. We see that as the Beloved reveals itself in its majesty and wonder, we realize the depth dimension of our being, the luminous expanse beyond color and concept that functions as the source of all other dimensions and forms of spiritual nature. The path of the heart is poetic and devotional, yet it ushers us into the full awakening of spirit.

All the experiences of true essential love explored in this trilogy are simply different ways in which we learn about the inherent goodness at the heart of all reality. It is the indestructible goodness that is potential for all of us.

A. H. ALMAAS
March 2022

Nondual Love

ONE

A New Dimension

In this book, we're going to explore what I call the boundless dimensions. They can also be called the formless dimensions or the dimensions of omnipresence. What this means is that we're going beyond the dimension of working with the individual soul. By individual soul I mean our individual consciousness—that which forms our subjectivity and is the carrier and site of all of our experiences and perceptions. It is consciousness located in space and time. To go beyond the individual soul requires some fundamental shifts in perception, and it's worth saying from the outset that the teaching on this can be difficult to grasp at first. Human language evolved to express the viewpoint of human beings as individuals, and using that language to describe a completely different perception of reality has its limitations.

So it may well be that this different account of reality just doesn't make sense at first because we're no longer looking at things from the viewpoint of the individual soul. When we're studying the soul and its various aspects, its gross and subtle faculties and its ordinary and spiritual qualities, we learn about the nature of the soul and the true nature of the individual. In that work, you study yourself and you discover different ways of experiencing yourself. When we're dealing with the boundless dimensions, we are discovering different ways of experiencing reality as a whole, not just our experience of ourselves. There's a shift of focus from the experience of the individual soul to the experience of the wholeness of existence. Now we are looking at the true nature of everything, the whole universe, which includes but goes beyond the physical universe.

To use religious terminology, we can work on understanding the soul, or we can work on understanding God, or the supreme being. To understand the nature of everything is to understand what the supreme being is, to understand the nature of God or the universal spirit. And when I use the terms "God," "divine being," or "supreme being" here, I don't mean an entity that lives in some heaven, that creates things in time and sends emissaries to reward or punish us or anything like that. If we think of it in that way, we're still looking from the viewpoint of the individual soul. In the boundless dimensions there are no separate entities, human or divine. One of the main barriers to understanding any of the boundless dimensions is insisting on experiencing yourself or the divine being as an entity that walks around in space and time and does things to other entities. Some people maintain that God created space and time, but they also see God as having legs and walking and talking and all that. But how can God have legs and walk and talk *and* create space and time? God needs space and time to walk and talk.

Of course, people do have experiences or visions of a form of divine presentation, like a figure sitting on a throne and that kind of thing. These things can happen, but that's not what I mean here by the divine or supreme presence and boundless dimensions. I mean it in the sense of a complete transcendence of individual human experience. It may take years, but our work on the boundless dimensions will eventually show us the true richness of the universe, revealing how the physical universe that humans normally see is only one thin layer of a multileveled, multidimensional universe.

Now, one of the challenges in approaching the boundless dimensions is that as you go deeper and deeper into them, there's less and less in it for you, as you are no longer the central part of the picture. Once people see that, they often wonder why anyone would want to go there, and what the point of it all is. However, part of the intelligence and compassion of the divine being is that it frequently presents its nature at the beginning in a way that is attractive and accessible to human beings. This is through the quality of love. And so we begin with the first boundless dimension, which I call the dimension of Divine Love. It is easiest to open to because it is closest to our usual human experience. The word "love" means that it still feels familiar to the human being; it makes sense to the individual soul and is something we appreciate. This, of course, implies there are other boundless dimensions besides that of love, such as presence or awareness, for example.

Human beings relate to love easily. Just say the word "love" and everybody's happy. Say "will" or "power" and people get scared. So, the divine being is very smart. If we imagine it as a speaking being, it might say, "Well, let's give them love. That should be easy, since everybody feels deprived of it. It makes everybody feel safe and secure, and they can relax and not feel they have to resist it." We will see that notions of surrendering, of letting go, of relaxation, and of receiving grace and blessings are some of the familiar concepts of duality we draw on in an attempt to understand and approximate the experience of nondual divine love and how it functions.

We call this dimension Divine Love because there is a soft quality of lovingness in it. There's a tenderness, a gentleness, and a sweetness. It is an appreciative quality, a happy, joyful, light, and celebrative quality. It's comforting. All these qualities of lovingness make it attractive and approachable. Nevertheless, we will see that there are reasons why people can feel resistance toward it. This is *divine* love after all, not the kind of love we're familiar with. The divine element brings in a host of questions that the individual soul doesn't understand and as a result it can arouse fear.

So why do we call this love divine and think of it as a boundless dimension? In one sense, it's divine because it's not the kind of love that you feel person to person, toward somebody else; this nondual love transcends the subject/object dichotomy. But the notion of divinity isn't because it is related to something called God. It's the quality of the love itself that gives it divinity, the quality of consciousness in it. There's a human quality of consciousness and there's an animal quality, but there's also a divine quality.

This quality directly reveals the fundamental benevolence of reality. When it is experienced as an aspect of presence affecting us as individual souls, we call it living daylight because of its palpable goodness, similar to the positive impact that sunlight has on all life on Earth. It evokes in the soul a basic trust in the goodness of reality—a sense of safety, of relaxation, of support in the loving embrace of the universe. As a boundless dimension, it is a flowing, gentle, and holding presence of love that is exceptionally fine and delicate, touching us with its sense of purity. The complete purity of this love has an exquisiteness and refinement that is hard to describe. It's a pure, selfless, and completely motiveless kind of love and so exquisitely subtle and refined that it's difficult to call it anything but divine.

This divine quality gives the love an incredible softness and gentleness, as well as an amazing beauty and sense of harmony. Its boundlessness is evident in the way this exquisite, delicate, soft, graceful, harmonious sense of sweetness and presence comes through everything. It comes through the walls and fills the air. It holds Earth, it holds the whole universe, pervading everything, constituting everything. It is omnipresent—it is literally everywhere and in everything. It is not somebody's love. When we say "divine love," we mean it's the love of the divine being, and the divine being holds the whole universe. So the whole universe, all of physical reality, including human and all other beings, is experienced as this exquisite sense of purity, which is fresh and intensely sweet at the same time. This love has a warmth and coziness to it, which we could say is similar to what lovers experience, but it has a quality that transports us beyond that, bringing a lightness, as well as a sense of release and freedom.

To experience divine love is to recognize the presence of divinity everywhere—divinity as love, as a presence, as radiance. It's like the soft, golden light that you see when sunlight comes into a room in the late afternoon. Take that quality of golden light and then imagine it actually shining out of all the objects around you, including people's physical bodies, so that they look as if they are nothing but the substance of this light. They are glowing with its beauty. It's an exquisite kind of perception, an exquisite way of being.

The extreme softness and delicacy of divine love means that when it touches something, it can only melt it. You may notice your experience sometimes when you touch something very delicate and soft—you yourself tend to soften and relax and let go. It's like that, but this delicate softness touches you from all over, inside and out. There's a sense of pleasure and deliciousness, and a melting and surrender. We can call it letting go, or surrender, but all that means is that we are being melted by the grace of this presence. Generally, everyone yearns for the experience of uniting with this boundless and immense wholeness, with its exquisite lovingness. Everybody some place in their soul yearns and longs for this realization—wanting the experience of uniting with the oneness that is boundlessness, immensity, and the most exquisite lovingness. Being held in the gentlest, the safest, the most nourishing and caring way possible. We long for that and can imagine that when it happens it will bring total release, complete freedom, and utter carefreeness.

But there's a paradox here. Remember, the boundless dimensions are also called the formless dimensions, and to experience them is to know that there are no forms to hold them. This brings up various questions and apparent conflicts that we need to see, penetrate, and understand. Because even the language we've been using so far is a trap. To talk about being melted and surrendering is a trap. To talk about letting go is a trap. Why? Because from the perspective of divine love, there is only divine love. There's only this presence of complete purity and lovingness, of harmony, exquisiteness, and sweetness. In this nondual love, there is nobody there to let go. So who's going to surrender to whom?

But in transitioning to selflessness, it feels that way. In going from the usual experience of the human being to the experience of this boundless dimension of Divine Love, we try to explain the process as one of "letting go," "surrendering," "melting," "disappearing," "merging," or "uniting with." These are all terms that we use, and in later chapters we'll see that at many stages of the journey it's pragmatic to view the transition in this way—it refers to the truth of where we are at those stages. So when we focus on our approach to divine love, we will see our encounter with it as involving us melting and surrendering because that makes sense to us at that stage. But if we really want to understand the dimension of Divine Love, we should keep in mind the limitations of such notions and remember that they are attempts to refer to something that they actually fail to describe. And for now, I'm going to describe things as they really are, even though it's not easy to capture the truth of reality in language.

The very fact that we experience the universe as being filled with physical objects, including our own bodies, which have weight, opaqueness, and solidity, is because we're not seeing the pervasiveness of divine love and the formlessness of the boundless dimensions. When we're open to the experience of divine love, we recognize that from its perspective there isn't really a physical universe the way we think of it. What we think of as the physical universe is nothing but a limitation of perception, because the universe is nothing but light and love. There are actually no rocks. Rocks don't exist; they can only be experienced.

Now this is a part of the teaching that may well be difficult to decipher, but it's important to understand what it's saying—namely, that the way we experience the world, as this physical universe with living entities in it, is the result of *experiencing things* instead of perceiving the true beingness that is really there. You see, God doesn't experience anything; God *is* everything. It's we who experience things—we have experience—and that is one of the main barriers to the perception of divinity and boundlessness. That's what I mean when I say that a rock, and by that I mean any physical object, doesn't really exist. It can only be experienced. Its existence as a separate object is not fundamental, and this is true in all of the boundless dimensions.

As long as there is experience, there are physical objects. So, you might say, "Oh, you mean, like, there should be no experience, and then there could be the perception of divinity?" Yes. But wait and see what I mean. If you want to go with me here, you have to be patient. We're dealing with one of the first barriers that arises in the transition to the boundless dimensions, and that is the concept of experience. Not what kind of experience you can have but the very notion of experience itself.

We normally think of it in this way: For there to be an experience, there must be somebody there having the experience. You believe that if you're not there as an individual consciousness, then whatever is there won't be experienced, yes? That's the usual understanding, and it means that the concept of experience is completely bound up with the concept of you as an individual existence. We only think of living entities having experiences, right? You don't say the universe has an experience. So the moment you imagine this living entity not being there, you think, "How could there still be experience?" Because, well, who's going to have the experience?

In a very subtle way we are all operating according to this concept of experience and buying into it all the time. We've never really thought about it, because that's what we've always known: "I go from one experience to another, of course. I'm always experiencing something, and for there to be an experience, there has to be an experiencer, who is somebody." Nobody would argue with that. If there's any argument, it's whether it's possible for it to be otherwise. But in the boundless dimensions it's otherwise, which is why they're difficult for most people to penetrate. And as I've said, even our language isn't fit for the purpose here—it's deceptive. I just said that these dimensions are difficult for people to penetrate, which means there are these entities who do something, which is penetrate, right? Well, it isn't really like that, but our language isn't set up to describe God's sense of perception. We don't have a divine language. Human languages are constructed to describe the experiences of human beings who walk around experiencing and believing themselves to be individual entities, basically individual bodies, or physical objects capable of locomotion.

Now, you might have a boundless experience once in a while. You experience the boundlessness, and you feel everything as one. However, it doesn't last very long. And one of the reasons it doesn't last is because you believe it's an experience you're having. The moment you think that, the experiencer reasserts itself as an individual entity, who now thinks, "Wasn't that an amazing experience?" But the experience of boundlessness is not what we usually mean by "experience," because the sense of it is not like, "I'm there, having one experience and then another experience." In the boundlessness of divine love, at some point the experiencer recognizes, "Oh, this is all delusion—there is no experiencer." And then the experiencer is gone, and there is only what is. There is awareness; there is perception and consciousness, because divine love is consciousness, it is light. But there is nobody having the experience. It's more like, "Oh. That's how things are. This is reality." Reality is conscious of itself, because it is consciousness, but it's not an experience happening to somebody.

It's like the one who is having experiences quits. Then there is the perception of what's there all the time—you don't call that an experience, do you? Would you call the presence of this room an experience? Or is it just there? It's just a room. You believe that if you leave, it will still be there. That's what the dimension of Divine Love is. You might leave it, meaning you become an individual again, but that doesn't mean it's gone. You are the one who comes and goes. After leaving the boundless dimension, you could refer to it from memory and say, "I had the experience of boundlessness," but then you've gone back to being an experiencer having experiences. If you stay in the boundlessness, you don't say, "I'm having an experience." If there is experience, it's God's experience, and God doesn't need to say "my" because there's only God. For "my" to make sense, there must be "yours" and "theirs." But with God, well, there is no "yours." There is only this presence, this reality, this truth that is here. Experience belongs to nobody; it is as it is.

With *having* an experience on the other hand, there is always my experience, your experience, his experience, her experience. We cannot conceive of experience that is not related to somebody having that experience. So the notion of experience is inextricably linked with ownership. When you say, "I'm having an experience" or "You're having an experience," you're saying that the person owns that experience. See? This is something we tend not to be aware of; we take it for granted that experience is always owned by an experiencer. And that is why it's difficult for people to understand divine being. Because everybody then thinks that divine being or unity of existence has experiences, just like us. So we make divinity or supreme being into some kind of individual existence living in time and space that has a sense of ownership.

Because we may never have challenged this sense of experience always being owned, a major issue arises when the divine being begins to show itself to the individual. The individual thinks, "Oh, oh. I have to let go here. But if I let go, if I surrender, who's going to have the experience? I'm gonna miss out. I'm not gonna be around to enjoy it!" That becomes the struggle, you see. You might long for the union and oneness of the surrender, but then you worry that this surrender means it's not going to be your experience. It might be somebody else's, God's experience maybe, but it's not going to be yours. And then you think, "Oh no, I want the experience. I want to be the one who surrenders, and I want to be there for the union and the merging."

So the first thing that needs to be penetrated and understood here, that needs to be given up and metabolized, is our notion of having an experience. Because as we enter the dimension of Divine Love, it's not a matter of "Oh, here I am, about to have another experience, just like I've been having experiences all these years." Maybe all your experiences have been like that so far on this path; perhaps you've had deep experiences of essence and being and seeing the wonder and even experiencing divinity, right? So there you are, seeing God, or God talking to you or something like that. But to really go into the dimension of Divine Love is a whole different thing. It means this whole stream of having experiences is going to quit. It's like there's a program that's been running in your operating system, which is self-registering: I'm having experiences of various things—now this one, now this one, now another one, and now this one. Right? And then it comes to the point where that program is going to quit. It's not going to be registering any more perceptions. And the fear here is that there won't be any experience if that quits. Or if there is experience, it's not going to be mine.

It *is* somebody having an experience as long as the universe of consciousness is being funneled into a particular locus of consciousness. It's like the individual having an experience of the boundless dimension operates as a kind of sphincter, constricting the flow of universal consciousness into what feels like their own particular experience. But when that sphincter is completely relaxed and the funnel is dissolved, then there is only the presence that is there, which is universal consciousness, unconstricted. And at this level we recognize the quality of this consciousness as pure love. The closest thing we know to it as humans is love, though as I've said, this isn't love in the sense of loving somebody. It's consciousness, it's light, it's presence. But sweet.

We shift into a whole different universe. In a sense, we move from the physical universe to the heavenly universe. It doesn't mean you've gone anywhere. Heaven is not anywhere else, and God doesn't live in a heaven. God the divine being is nothing but the reality that we are always in, but without us having an experience of it. Reality being itself, conscious of itself, just as it is, and without it being funneled by a particular individual. So we can talk about an experience of reality, and think we're having one, but in truth it's a distortion. There is no experience of reality; there is just reality.

On the conventional level, however, there is just individual experience. As long as we think of ourselves as an individual soul, as this entity, this person with its own separate existence, it makes sense to talk about having experiences and then to talk about letting go, surrendering, and all these things. It works to some degree to look at things this way, and as I said, we'll be doing that in later chapters, because it can take us along the path toward divinity in a way that's easier for us to embrace in our normal lives. But I'm not approaching it that way here, and I want to make clear that there is ultimately a significant limitation to that approach. The problem is that we'll always be limited to experiences *with* divinity instead of the real realization *of* divinity.

What we have to deal with ultimately is a fear of the loss of our own experience, which is fear of the loss of individuality, separateness, personalness. And whether you've been experiencing individuality at the personality level or at the essential level as the personal essence, you might be afraid you're going to lose it. In truth, the surrender of experience is not a matter of surrendering your identity. It's not a matter of who you are as an individual but that you are an individual. It's not the surrendering of "I" but the surrendering of "my," which is in some sense a more difficult, subtler thing.

So if you lose your sense of having your own experience, it doesn't mean that you're going to lose your sense of autonomy, your independence. You think it does, because of that fundamental problem of not being able to differentiate experience from the concept of there being someone to have the experience. "How can I be independent if I don't have my own experience?" So everyone says, "I want to have *my* experience, my own experience." And yes, that's good to have for a while, but eventually we need to go further. At which point everyone says, "No, I want to continue having *my* experience. I'm going to experience God my way." Right?

It's really all a matter of a lack of understanding, which results in the lack of precision in the language used. We don't understand what reality is, so we don't understand how there can be existence, how there can be perception and life, without our usual notion of experience. If I let go of the sense of my individual experience and of being an individual experiencer, will there still be perception? Will it be mine? What will it be like? How am I going to live *my* life? We don't know, and that ignorance brings forth all these fears and concerns.

But consciousness exists without individual experience, without a separate individual having an experience. In the boundlessness of divine love, consciousness or presence is everywhere. It's everywhere in the way that space is everywhere, inside the physical, even inside the atoms. Nothing escapes it. There's no place where it isn't. And it is one, undivided wholeness. And within this ocean of loving consciousness, our personal presence is simply a further condensation—a denser, fuller drop of ocean nectar. The ocean of divine love remains undivided, and it is the very substance of this drop of nectar, which is never separate from the ocean of love.

PRACTICE SESSION
OWNERSHIP OF EXPERIENCE
. . .

In the following exercise, we'll explore the notion of owning your experience—by which I mean possessing it, having it be yours—by doing a form of exercise called a repeating question. If you are doing this exercise with someone else, you will ask your partner the first question over and over for fifteen minutes. Each time the question is asked, the person responding answers spontaneously with whatever arises for them. Answers may be a few words or many sentences—whatever needs to be said. After each response the person asking says, "Thank you" and then asks the question again. When the fifteen minutes are up, switch roles so the other person can answer the same question. Once you've both answered the first question, do the same with the second.

If you don't have a partner to do this with, you can answer the questions in writing as many times as possible within the allotted time. Or you can record the questions and have them delivered to you each time by your computer or device after you finish answering out loud.

What's right about owning your experience?

Tell me something that makes your experience be your experience.

. . . . .

Questions and Comments

Student: I have two comments. For the first question, what came up for me was that there are different selves in me that each have their own experiences, and if I switch from one self to another, I have a totally different way of seeing the world. And I get confused as to who's owning the experience. Which self is it? And then for the second question, what came up is that what seemed to make it my experience was contactfulness. Without that, there would be some separation. But if I had that experience directly, there would be a contactfulness there, but that contactfulness itself had a quality of boundlessness. It seemed to be more awareness rather than experience.

A. H. Almaas: Makes sense, yes. The more you're not holding on to the sense of individual experience, the more you feel it as an awareness. It won't feel like you're having an experience. It will feel like there's a perception of reality rather than an inner experience. When you close your eyes and then open them and see the building, are you having an inner experience? No, you're just seeing what's there. So when the concept of experience is not operative, what's there is just perception. And the first question was?

S: It's about the different selves. That each self seems to have its own experience. It's like there's some confusion about who owns these experiences.

AH: I'm sure, yes. It's not only whether it's your experience or not, but which one of you owns it, right? So when you see that there are different selves in you that perceive what your experience is and naturally think they own it, then there's the possibility of unification, so that there's only one person having the experience. And then after that it's possible to go beyond that, beyond the experiencer.

S: I got to the stage where I just felt I was a point, and it feels like that's what creates experience. That's what separates awareness into being able to experience itself, and it also seems like I'm bound by it, so that I don't have a way to get outside of "I," at least from this place I'm at right now.

AH: Yes. That makes sense. You don't have a way of getting out of the experiencer. It's not just you in particular having difficulty with this, it's a universal thing. The experiencer cannot get out of being an experiencer. That's why the only possibility is grace. Which means divine love itself manifests and dissolves your sense of being the separate experiencer. All you can do is understand the situation as thoroughly as possible. That way, you don't cooperate in resisting divine love. However, the sense of yourself as a point doesn't have to be the way you are saying it. The point can be a pure simple witnessing of what occurs, without the witness being separate from the witnessed. The point is one way of experiencing pure consciousness or presence, and if you let yourself be that, it is bound to transform you into a boundless infinite consciousness.

S: It seemed to me that as a little baby I was just floating in a field of multidimensional experience, without even necessarily having any memory of it happening. And then through learning language and fixating and discriminating, memory was created. And as I create a broader and broader base of memory, with all its language, in effect I'm creating a broader and broader self. And that creates the structure. And through the identification with that warehouse of memory, when something arises I'm labeling it out of my memory. That identification with that process seems to be how I create my experience as mine.

AH: Makes sense. So you're seeing the process through which the individual experiencer develops.

One important point in what you said is that at the beginning you were this baby floating in this multidimensional reality, right? Well, the experience that you are a baby floating in this multidimensional reality is partly created by the experiencer. You are the multidimensional reality and the baby is only your sense of "I." You see? We usually think we are that, you see. That identity that we are the baby, or the body, or whatever, is one of the initial things that develops the sense of a separate experiencer.

S: When I tried to find out what makes my experience my experience, there were two ways that came up that seem to be contradictory. The first one seems to be on the superficial level, that when I share my experience and get validation from outside, that's how I try to make it my experience. But sometimes my experience can really feel like it's mine, and then it doesn't feel like it needs any sharing. There's usually a sense of aloneness with that but total sureness. It's more like a state where I would perceive the noise in the room, or whatever, but there would also be aloneness. Not loneliness, but aloneness.

AH: Aloneness. That's true. So as you go through that, as you recognize the experiencer, and your own experiencer recognizes there's no need to share it, you feel the aloneness. The aloneness is a real thing here, and it's a transition. Alone doesn't mean that you're lonely; you're just accepting an existential situation. The desire to share and the feeling of aloneness both reflect the truth that you are not that separate experiencer, but they are interpreted through its filter. Which tells you that if you are an individual, separate experiencer, then there are other ones too who you could share things with, right? And also that you can be alone. However, if you are the boundless divine presence, what does it mean to share your experience? There's no need, really, to share it then. Not because of the absence of feeling that need but because it just doesn't make sense. And aloneness is also a concept that does not fly anymore. So sharing is you wanting connection, which is really a reflection of wanting boundless love. That's why we always want to share, because boundless love is our real nature, so the longing for it comes from some deep place. It gets expressed in all kinds of ways of communicating, sharing, and having intimacy. But as we go deeper, we begin to experience the aloneness, and the aloneness can be the transition then to that state of boundlessness.

S: I found that I made an experience my experience and owned it as my mind wrapped around whatever the phenomena was. So, as I looked at my partner's eyes and thought them attractive or saw them moving, that caused a certain thought process to click off really rapidly in my head. It tied me into the experience and made it mine. It separated me from the experience. It made me here, and the experience out there. To the extent that I could relax that process and allow the experience to be pure, without my conceptualizing mind intervening, it felt that the separation between me and the experience disappeared. And then I became the experience rather than possessing it or being the experiencer in relation to the experience. So it was a very different phenomenon then. A barrier seemed to relax in my process.

AH: So the experiencer is not separate from the experience. But is there an experiencer in that experience? When you become the experience?

S: The experiencer certainly was less definitive. There was less of the experiencer. It became much more like just an experience on its own.

AH: Right. See, the thing about the conceptual process that goes on in the head, about seeing the other person, all this mental processing . . . there is implicit in that process the conceptualization of an experiencer. There is you, and there is the other person. And you're thinking about you relating to the other person. That moment of thinking is generating you as an individual separate person who is relating to this person and having an experience. So that's why when the thought process gets quieter, we lose that sense of separateness. But it's not really just the fact of thinking. There are specific things implicit in the thoughts; there is content, and the content is that there is you relating to somebody else. That's really what creates the separateness, not just the fact of thinking by itself. Because if you could think without implicitly taking these ideas to be true, you could think without the sense of the experiencer.

S: It felt to me like there were extremely rapid little firings of thought, looking out into, say, the volume of the space here. I couldn't catch most of them. Once in a while one would settle, but for the most part it just went *burrrrrrrrrrrrr*.

AH: So you had a glimpse of this background of thinking, which it's true, is like that. It's very fast; it's going on all the time.

S: And that's what makes the experiencer. And holds it in place.

AH: Exactly. That's why we say it's a mental creation. The mind's actually doing that.

S: I'm having a hard time with this whole concept. I found that I was really angry. I was angry at you, and I was angry at the concept of divine love and God. I was raised in a Jewish family, and I guess I grew up with all the fear that I was exposed to in that environment. And I have a difficult time believing that there's a nurturing energy out there that I'm part of and that will take care of me. That I can trust in and let go of my boundary and sense of individuality. And I hear you talking about letting go and having holding, you know, and nurturing love and merging energy, and I just, I'm not with you. I just don't know where I fit in the universe based on what you're talking about.

AH: Very good point. I'm sure there are other people probably feeling similar things about this divine love business: "I don't see any divine love. I've been doing it all by myself without much help and most of the time it sucks." That's something the question of divine love and boundlessness will bring up for many people— the question of basic trust and holding. You may have seen this already in relationship to your early holding environment and your sense of trust in whether the world is safe. But it will come up again here, because it's particularly related to divine love. And what will also come up with it is anger and a feeling of hatred toward the idea of divine love. When we're invited to see the truth of the goodness of the universe, that it is nothing but divine love, it can obviously make us very aware of our feeling of total disconnection from this and the sense of deprivation and abandonment our history may have left us with. This manifests in what we usually call the issue of the beast. When the beast is active, it's not just that you don't believe divine love exists; even if you see it, you hate it. Even if divine love shows itself to you, the immediate reaction is an angry feeling of "Where have you been all this time?"

S: What is this issue with the beast?

AH: The beast arises when the personality of the individual is relating to the idea of God as a person, and it has the same dynamic as a young child relating to its mother. If a young child feels abandoned by its mother for long enough, then even if she returns full of love, the child's first response is often one of angry rejection. In the same way, if we feel that God wasn't there when we were suffering, and we therefore felt abandoned, when God's love finally shows up, we hate it. We oppose it and say we don't want it. There's a level of not trusting that there is such a thing as this love, not believing in it because we've felt bitterly disappointed by it. But there's also a level of not *wanting* to believe in it and actually wanting to destroy it, so we don't have to risk the vulnerability that comes with our dependence on it. So the beast opposes the light, opposes the love itself. And that's fine, that's part of what arises, and it needs to be allowed its space, without being acted out.

S: Well, I guess I still doubt if there is a reality that's beyond everybody, you know. At least beyond my understanding. Because then, what's the reality of something like a holocaust or Bosnia or

Rwanda or any of the horrible things that happen to good people, or people that believe in God or some kind of spirit in the world?
AH: Yes, that's true. That all happens. And one of the main reasons it happens is that everybody goes around believing they are separate, independent experiencers who need to protect themselves and own their territory and want to expand their territory. If people recognized that they're not really independent, separate selves, that it's all one living reality, I don't think people would do that to each other.
S: That I can understand.
AH: So that's really a very direct consequence. The more you see yourself as an independent, separate island, the more scared you are and the more you want to protect yourself. And then the protection becomes an attack. Then hatred, divisiveness, and enmity will arise. So divine love helps with these things. That's why divine love is sometimes called Christ love. Because it dissolves all these boundaries and this separateness. It shows that we're all one, really.

S: I was really struck by the paradox in the first question, about owning my experience. And I realized that the owning had such a quality of permanence to it, and the experience had such a quality of ephemerality to it. And how all of these transitory experiences, I actually gave a kind of substantiality to them in terms of taking that to be my identity. And there's a sort of paradox in this. Because how can all these ephemeral things create a permanent sense of self?
AH: Yes, it is an interesting paradox. It's the same thing with divine presence. Divine presence is always a boundless, infinite, completely loving and conscious presence. But that divine presence can limit itself, right, by beginning to look through one pair

of eyes, and then identify with that. It can identify with one body to the extent that it forgets who it is really.

But there's something I want to emphasize here. When I talked about divine love and how it transcends all boundaries, I wasn't saying that *you* should try to transcend these boundaries. I did not give any exhortation to give up your separateness, your separate self. We're only working on understanding it, we're only inquiring into it. Remember what I said: The individual entity, the separate individual, cannot get out of its place. That's why I wouldn't tell you how to do it. We can only understand. And circumstances might happen in your life in a certain way, divine love might arise in a particular way for you, to show you its truth. So you can only inquire and understand, and by understanding you will harmonize yourself with the truth that you see. You don't need to do anything; nobody's going to ask you to do anything. Your own understanding will unfold your experience wherever it goes, so it will feel congruent with you. It's not something you have to give up when you don't want to give it up. And as long as you don't want to give it up, you're not going to give it up. You only give it up when you recognize and understand that it doesn't really exist. You realize you were believing something that was untrue. And then it doesn't even feel like giving it up; you just change your mind, in a sense. It's an experience of a conversion of sorts.

S: What I was looking at was about recognizing my own experience. When I'm present with my experience, I have an intuitive sense that it's mine. But there seems to be a deeper soul level, for example, if I go to a retreat and I go through all my ups and downs, and I recognize, "Ah, that's my fixation or this is my particular path through this, which other people have in a different way." That seems to be one level of it. And, actually, recognizing that, even though it's these fixations and stuff, I recognize I get closer to myself because I'm more conscious of it. And then another example is when I recognize a particular way in which something like a movie or something affects me, and I feel like I'm in touch with my guidance, or a certain way that my soul is unfolded and impacted by the experience. And then I might go into something like, "Oh. I'm special. I'm validated. I'm having this experience, this is me." And I can go on that way. And then I'm following a thread. And there's an inner part of that thread where I let go of that need for validation, and I'm in touch with a deeper kind of guidance or unfolding. And it's full, so I don't need to self-reference, "Oh, this is me and I'm special" and all of that. I mean, there's still an experiencer there, but it becomes much more transparent. So, to me the thread through all of this is a sense of a certain way that I recognize the divine is manifesting, unfolding the soul in my case, in a sense.

AH: You have to own your experience first, you see. You have to recognize it, own it, and live it before you can go beyond it. Because basically, owning and acknowledging your experience is recognizing your essential nature. But as you recognize your essential nature, you realize at some point that your essential nature is also the essential nature of everything. So when you recognize that, you realize, "Oh, it's not my experience." But the way you described it, that's how the process works.

S: This brought me to the subject of memory. Because you've talked about your experience of the boundless dimension in your book *Luminous Night's Journey*. And I wonder, was there any memory of that afterward? Because it seems like when you move into a boundless space, if you lose the sense of mine, this is where I get stuck; I want to be able to move into such a space and come back remembering it. So I can't get beyond "this is mine." I did once have an experience in a private session where I suddenly felt like I had lost consciousness. And when I came to I realized that I had forgotten that there was a me, somehow, and I had ceased to exist. But I couldn't remember what happened beyond that point. Just the ceasing existing.

AH: Well that happens, yes. There's a certain kind of situation where you cease to exist. And when you cease to exist, of course you don't remember because there's nothing to remember. And nobody there to remember anything. So it's not like you don't remember. It's more like there was no content to be remembered.

S: So then it brings me to the subject of motivation. And I can't be motiveless. If I'm without motive, why bother?

AH: If you're really without motive, you will see only the divine presence. Not having a conscious motive doesn't mean you don't have a motive. You probably have millions of motives, even when you feel you don't have a motive. People who are sort of apathetic and unmotivated, those people have lots of very deep motives. They're just not aware of them, they're suppressed. Somebody who's really motiveless, right, is somebody who is realized.

TWO

The Dimming of the Light

When our soul is open to the dimension of Divine Love, we begin to experience our true nature, free from limitations. Before that, we may experience our true nature as essential presence, but we experience it as inside our body, as the inner nature of the soul. In the dimension of Divine Love, we begin to experience our nature closer to what it really is. It's now free from the limitation of the ego principle, the term we use for the identification with being a limited entity, a bounded individual. The term "ego principle" sounds modern and Western, but it's just one way of translating the ancient Sanskrit term *ahamkara*. It's the way most people experience themselves, and it's nothing esoteric. It's how the soul experiences itself when it is imprinted by the ego structure: "I am this person, this separate individual, who was born and now lives, and I do this and do that, and I interact with other people, who are also separate and different from me. I have my uniqueness, and they have their own uniqueness. We can interact and share or fight and all that." That is the basis of the ego principle, the ahamkara.

As we penetrate through that, as we're able to experience our essential nature without that limitation (which is simply a construction of mind that has become habitual), we experience our true nature in slightly different ways, depending on which one of the boundless dimensions is revealing itself. In the dimension we are exploring, we realize that instead of consciousness or awareness, our true nature is divine love, which can be experienced as love, as presence, or as light. How we experience it depends on which of our three subtle centers is dominant. We experience it as presence if the belly center is dominant, as love if the heart center is dominant, and as light if the head center is dominant. It's all one thing, however; they're not separate, with different characteristics. Reality is presence, the presence itself can express itself as love, and the love itself is the light. And it is divine because it is free from the limitation of the ego perspective. There is the recognition that my nature, what I am, is no different from what reality is, this infinite undivided ocean of pure loving light that is existence or presence.

The light can manifest itself in various degrees of intensity—it can be dimmer or brighter. The more intense and brighter the light is, the more you will see the reality of how things are. The less intense and dimmer the light is, the more obscured and inaccurate your perception will be. This light or love or presence generally manifests more intensely in human beings than it does, for instance, in rocks or trees. But even in human beings it manifests in various degrees of purity, intensity, and brilliance. When it manifests in a human being dimly, the dimness of the light means that this being experiences itself as a limited separate individual. Everything looks separate because the boundaries of things, their surfaces, become less transparent; they are dense and opaque to this light because it isn't so intense. The surface of things becomes more dominant in that person's perception of reality and therefore more important. Eventually the partition between things becomes so predominant that the person believes they are this limited entity sitting there in their separate body in a world full of separate people and physical objects.

But if this light intensifies in the location of the body, it better penetrates through these surfaces and boundaries. And the more it does that, the more it reveals that these surfaces are ultimately not opaque; the light is actually present all the way through them. So when the light is dim, we have the conventional experience of the ego. When the light is bright, we have what is called a buddha, or a realized individual. It's the same light in both, the same presence, the same consciousness and beingness, but different degrees of it can result in very different perceptions of reality.

So even though this divine effulgence of light goes all the way through everything and is oozing out of everywhere, as it dims in my location I stop seeing it. I begin to see only objects and people, as separate things. However, because this light is inherent in our nature, our innate sense of being rooted in that omnipresent ocean of divine light, love, and consciousness does not completely disappear. It manifests then, when we are still open to it, as love for someone else or love for something such as nature. When we experience it as love for another, it is nothing but a reflection of the fact that we and the other are one, made out of the same love, but perceived through the limitation of a boundary that says we're two.

The boundary between the two people, however, is no longer so dense and opaque, and divine love emerges through the heart, as that is the easiest place for this presence to emerge in us. We call what arises love. In our individual experience, it manifests in different qualities—for example, as pink love or merging love. Pink love is a personal love or liking for somebody or something. It's characterized by softness and tenderness, with an appreciation for the beauty that we see in another's unique individual expression of reality. Merging love is the delicious state in which the structures and boundaries that cause the feeling of separation between two souls—or between us and our own source—relax and melt.

However, if we're stuck in our belief in the ego principle, in the concept of being a separate individual entity, the boundaries remain opaque. The light is dim and the love is not there. But then we experience the longing for love, a longing to be one with somebody else. There is a desire for contact, closeness, sharing, and togetherness; a yearning for intimacy and merging. And this is all because we don't recognize that we are already one with the other. So I say I want to share myself with you. What do I mean by "share myself"? I am you. How can I share myself with you? My wanting to share myself with you, us wanting to share with each other, is motivated by the fact that unity underlies all our experience. There is a desire to share because this unity is being expressed through duality. It's being perceived through the filter of the ego principle, which thinks there are two people who can share and that by sharing, maybe love will emerge and bring us closer together.

Because we're not aware that our true nature is this boundless omnipresent effulgence of pure love and light, when we have something we like, we become attached to it. We become possessive. If there is somebody you love, you're attached to them. Any object you love, you become attached to. So what is attachment?

It's a substitute for divine love. Attachment is a way of trying to get the feeling that I am one with this: I have it now, it's mine, and it can't leave me. If you recognize the dimension of Divine Love, you know that you and the object are all one thing, so you don't need to hold on to it. But since you don't know consciously that it's all one thing (you only know it unconsciously), you believe you are a separate thing that can have something else. And so we develop attachments. We're bound to develop attachments; it's our way to preserve the closeness and connection.

But if we explore attachment, we recognize that it is in fact a negativity, the result of a frustration of the heart. We can see that attachment is a negative kind of merging—it's not real merging. It's a desire for the state of divinity, for this divine love that is everywhere, but it's frustrated by the sense of boundaries. We are this unity, which is beautiful and harmonious, liberated and complete, so when we are experiencing ourselves as something limited and constricted, we can't help longing for that unity. If our obscuration is somewhat light, we experience it as a longing for union with the divine, with God. If our obscuration is a little thicker, we experience it as a longing to unite with somebody else. If our obscuration is even thicker, we experience it only as frustration—frustrated desire. Attachment means you are having divine love without having it—the ego believes it achieves unity that way, but it doesn't really have it. In a state of attachment, although you are holding on to something you think you want, inside the attachment is frustration because you're not getting what you really want—the loving union.

So that's why all spiritual techniques have to do with intensifying the glow at the location of your soul; intensifying the brilliance, the light, the awareness of the soul. Different traditions have different ways of explaining how the light dims in a certain location. The yogic Hindu tradition, for example, talks about the ahamkara principle and all the impressions and tendencies in the soul that come from past experiences. These tend to predispose you toward things similar to those impressions.

If you're a Christian, then the concept used is sin, original sin, the Fall, and all the passions that result from it. The way of intensifying the light is then through the virtues, which lead to redemption. You work with the impurities of the soul—what I call the blamable qualities.

If you're a Buddhist, then you use the understanding of the three poisons: ignorance, attachment, and aversion. Each one of these mushrooms into the various negative traits. And if we use our modern psychology as a way to understand it, we can say that it is the development of the ego structure and our identification with it that obscures this inner light.

These are all stories, attempts to describe and understand how the light dims, and none of them is completely accurate. All we know is that the light dims or gets brighter. That we know for sure. Every culture, every era, has had its own way of explaining it. Maybe two hundred years from now there will be a completely different way of explaining it, which will be meaningful for that particular time. So whatever understanding of the human psyche we use, when we combine it with the idea of the dimming and brightening of the light, techniques will be developed for intensifying the light.

If the light is not dimmed, your sense of who you are has the quality of divine love; a very light, bright, and empty quality, which is also soft, delicate, and melted at the same time. I've described how this divine loving light is everywhere, and everything is manifesting out of it—it's all one thing. This one thing can recognize itself even as it manifests in the form of an individual, but only if that individual form embodies the essence of the pure light. And we've seen that one of the things that creates the dimming of that light is the ego principle—the belief in being a separate individual soul on your own. That's what Buddhism calls the self, and it is our usual view of ourselves. From that perspective, instead of divine love still recognizing itself in a certain form, the person recognizes themself only as this separate entity that moves in time and space. From the perspective of divine love, that person doesn't really exist, because everything is actually love, light, and presence.

In the previous chapter I looked at how this sense of separate individuality leads to the idea of personal experience, having your own experience, which is one of the ways the ego principle dims the light. I'm looking now at another way the dimming occurs because of how we experience things, and that is attachment. In all of your experience there is an element of attachment. You are attached to the good thing and you want to hold on to it; the bad thing, you want to push away. In both cases the ego principle is at work, believing that there is me and there is the other. I can hold on to the other or push them away. If you hold on to them, you create your own family, your own tribe. If you push them away, you create enemies and the like, and wars start.

So that's how attachment operates as a kind of negative merging. When our light is dimmed by the ego principle and its sense of ownership, the desire for merging and union with the divine turns into attachment. Attachment is a substitute form of merging—one with frustration inherent in it—and it's the only merging the ego is capable of. Even the notion of wanting union, longing for union, reflects your belief in the ownership of experience and the attachment it brings. It is "your" union with the divine that you want, and you are attached to that idea. So, we're going to explore this further now by doing an exercise on attachment.

PRACTICE SESSION
ATTACHMENT
· · ·

In this exercise you will work with one or two other people if possible. Each person in the group will do a monologue for fifteen minutes. If you are alone, you can write out your exploration for fifteen minutes. The idea is to express—either verbally or in writing—whatever comes up spontaneously, without censoring anything. You maintain an attitude of curiosity and interest in whatever appears and keep exploring to see if you can discover more about it. It may be an expression of ideas, feelings, or physical sensations that you are having, or a mixture of the three.

In the monologue, you want to explore your attachments to merging and union and how these manifest in your life. The attachment may be a desire to hold on to the experience of merging. And even if there is a desire to push it away, that is still an attachment. Maybe you can shed some light on how this attachment is based on the idea of duality between you as a separate individual soul and the other as a separate entity from you, even if the other is the divine, or God, or reality. You want to see your attachments and explore them until you see the ahamkara principle at work—the belief in duality, of there being a you and the other. Because without that duality, there wouldn't be any attachment. We've seen that attachment becomes one of the major barriers to knowing divine love, because it is a way that the ego creates a substitute for it.

· · · · ·

Questions and Comments

Student: As I was exploring that sense of wanting to merge and the frustration of not being able to do it, I saw that there's just this continual attempt to merge with people or things, or take them inside of me. And I realized there's no way that's ever going to happen. And that made me realize what you were saying at a very deep level. That as long as I think there is a me and another, I will continue to create this cycle of desire.

A. H. Almaas: Right. Very good. Exactly. A cycle of suffering.

S: Can the experience of the personal essence, or the pearl, get in the way of this?

AH: The experience of the pearl itself doesn't. To be the pearl, the personal essence, is to be an individual on the essential level. Developing this unique personal essence means that you can be a human being and live in the world while still being an expression of the divine. That's different from the ego sense of being an individual, which is based on the past and all the self-images that have developed from that. And it's also based on being separate from everything else. But the personal essence isn't separate. If you experience divine love, you experience your personal presence as a condensation, as a drop of that divine love that is condensing out of that ocean, without being separate from it. At the beginning you experience the personal essence, the pearl, as if it is separate from everything else, because the ego principle is still present. Then the sense of being an individual person still exists, even though you're experiencing the incomparable pearl.

S: So at another level there isn't that feeling of ownership of the pearl experience?

AH: If there's any sense of ownership, it's more like it's you that's being owned—you don't own anything. In the dimension before Divine Love, there is a sense of ownership. It's only natural for us to feel it, and we can say that it's real in that dimension, even if that reality is partly determined by a limitation in perception. When you're living in that limited reality, you can't pretend that there's no ownership. You need to acknowledge your sense of ownership, because that's the truth then. See? So what happens when you recognize your attachment and the dynamic underlying that attachment? What happens? Does the attachment increase? What kind of thing happens?

S: Well, I realize that the attachment and the cycle of desire and suffering also serve my ego, they serve to keep it intact. In a way, there's a sense of security in the separateness. It sounds strange, but it's true. Because you haven't talked about death or annihilation yet in becoming everything. And I think my ego is very scared of that.

AH: Oh, yes. I think many egos here are scared of that right now. It might sound good, all this love, but everybody is wondering, and feeling paranoid, "Is God gonna get me now? Will there be a me left?"

S: This morning when you were talking, I kept wondering, "What is this density barrier that we have?" And I guess it's quite simply our ego and needing to feel separate. I guess from the day I was born I've been trying to be separate, and so it ends up all being "me," "mine," and "my." And I realize that the only thing I owned was my suffering. That any essential experience I've had doesn't have this sense of ownership to it. It's been there and I remember it; I haven't wiped it out.

AH: That's true, yes.

S: But it's only my suffering that I own.

AH: Yes. And that's one of the last things to go. One of the last holdouts, you see.

S: I realize that in the feeling of attachment to the other person there's an identity that goes along with it, that I'm a loser. And I don't have any idea how to be in a relationship with somebody else without having that dynamic be there. I don't have that dynamic when I'm alone. When I'm alone, I'm fine. But when I'm in relationship with someone, it seems like that's implied. So does anybody have a story about how to be in relationship with someone without that attachment and the longing and all the accompanying identities? I'd like to hear it.

AH: I'm sure there are many stories. But you know, whether you experience yourself as a loser or a winner, attachment's the same. Not only losers have attachments. Winners actually have more difficult attachments.

S: How can you be in relationship without attachment then?

AH: The more you know your true nature, and that your true nature is everywhere, the less you'll be attached.

S: I notice that I'm someone who's very much attached, always wanting to be with people. Wanting relationship, wanting. But what happened to me as I explored that is I felt, I became aware, that behind that was this desire for God. And it just felt really beautiful. I felt this really sweet quality, and it didn't matter to me that I was desiring all these things on the human level. It was just really beautiful and sweet.

AH: Exactly. That's what underlies attachment, really. It's a desire for God. If you don't recognize that, then there is frustration. If you're aware of your desire for God, then you recognize the love inherent in that. And that will bring the sweetness.

S: Something interesting coming up for me a lot in this whole exploration is perceiving myself or my ego as a kind of spatial configuration.

AH: Yeah.

S: And I've never experienced it quite that way before. As I started exploring I could see that there's my sense of myself, with memories and all that, which is like a shadow that's there, always present as I'm experiencing. And then there's the other side of that, which is there's other. There's myself and there's other. And that's like the obvious level. But then I started feeling that there's more to it, and it's that I'm in a particular place, like a location. And maybe it's like a time-space kind of place or something. And that keeps coming up. And it feels more powerful, more underlying than even the objects-relation aspect of that duality.

AH: That's very true. That's what I mean by structure, the ego structure. It's actually a spatial structure. You'll recognize that directly at some point. And it's as if that spatial structure sort of keeps everything out, including divine love.

S: What I noticed is that I would be with some of the attachments, and some expansiveness would start to happen and a kind of loosening. And there was a kind of disorientation that came with that. A certain freedom would begin to arise but then really quickly, it's like there would be this recognition of disorientation, and then I'd want to reconfigure spatially.

AH: I see, yes. It's good to go with the disorientation, to let yourself get disoriented. Because your orientation is through that structure, through that spatial, temporal location. As that structure begins to dissolve, melt, or relax, you start to experience disorientation. You might even actually get dizzy. So just sit down and let it happen. Don't fight it. You won't know what's happening for a while but that's the transition you have to go through. As long as you know what's happening, you still have control, you see, that structure has control. So there's a disorientation, a getting dizzy, you don't know what's going on. That's okay, you know, things melt. So that's true, that's how it happens. The more we talk about the pervasiveness of true nature, how it's everywhere, the more that puts pressure on the spatial quality of our structure. It exposes it.

S: I was trying to relate this exercise to just my real physicalness, because I've been in a lot of physical pain lately. So my attachments have to do with really seeing my attachment to the body and resistance to really being with the pain. And I was trying to relate that to this exercise, feeling like there was some similarity on the physical level to emotional stuff I've felt in the past. Resistance and attachment, but I'm not really very clear about it. I wonder if there's something you can say about this in relation to our physical bodies and pain? And our relationship with it.

AH: It's all the same thing. Attachment operates in two different ways—attraction or repulsion. If something's pleasurable we want to attract it, and we're attached to the attraction. But if it's painful, we're attached to the repulsion. It's the same thing whether it's the body or something else—attachment works the same way. Anyway, ego structure appears in the body as tension patterns, including surface tension at the skin, which is how the ego principle appears physically. Now, the more you experience yourself, the more you let yourself be aware and become present, the more you experience the physical pain, right? But it's possible that if you went to a more boundless dimension there would be less physical pain. Not exactly that it would be less, but you would be bigger.

S: Well it sometimes feels like the pain is just an interpretation of a sensation, which is actually just a different sensation. But there's this conditioned response to it—"This is wrong; I don't want it"—and I try to get rid of it. And sometimes, it's like, why am I doing this? Why don't I just let go and go into it, relax into the pain? It seems like that's a possibility.

AH: Yes, it is. And actually it's a good thing to experiment with. In the boundless dimension of love, pain and pleasure are simply variations or patterns of appearance in the ocean of conscious love.

THREE

The Whole Story

As we continue to explore this boundless dimension of Divine Love, it can be helpful to get a perspective on how it all fits into the bigger picture in the Diamond Approach. To better understand the language and system of any teaching, it can help to see it all put together sometimes—to get the whole story. So I'm going to do that now by outlining all the basic elements in the Diamond Approach that need to be understood both intellectually and experientially.

First of all, there's the ego, the experience of the personality, which is our conditioned historical self. Then there's the soul, our living consciousness, which includes the ego as a fixated structure within it. The ego self is a historical, mostly mental, structuring of the soul. The soul also includes our body—the physical manifestation or outer expression of the soul—and the way our living consciousness informs our physicality. We can say the soul animates the body, or follow Aristotle in saying that the body is the outer expression of the soul. Then there is what I call true nature, or the spiritual universe, which is the true ground of the soul. So we can say that the soul is the bridge between the ego and true nature, and also between the body and reality that is beyond the physical.

In the Diamond Approach, true nature consists of three elements: the essential aspects, the diamond vehicles, and the boundless dimensions. (There are other different manifestations of true nature in the Diamond Approach, but these are subtle and not commonly known and are beyond what we are discussing here.) All are experienceable forms of our essential nature. In this path, the essential aspects are most often the initial entrance into the spiritual universe. They reflect the fact that essence doesn't manifest with just one quality, and the variations of its manifestations give rise to the many different essential qualities, such as compassion, love, will, and truth. Each aspect has precise and definite experienceable characteristics—color, taste, and texture—and each has a particular psychological significance.

The diamond vehicles are bodies of knowledge, or structures of consciousness, that transmit to us particular dimensions of wisdom that are needed at different stages of the inner journey. They are like hard disks, and each one contains an amazing amount of experiential information about reality. One example is the diamond guidance, which helps us understand how the essential aspects are harmonized and integrated in our personal unfoldment. Another is the Markaba, which shows us that truth and pleasure are one and the same thing, though the pleasure is not the kind of gratification that the soul habitually seeks.[*]

And then we also work with the boundless dimensions, which reveal to the soul true nature as the transcendent ground

---

[*] See my book *Inner Journey Home* for more information about the diamond vehicles.

of reality. Each one refers to a particular way of experiencing this ground that permeates all of manifestation. There are five of these dimensions, including the one we're exploring here, Divine Love. The other four are the Supreme (where the ground is presence), the Nonconceptual (where the ground is awareness), the Absolute (where the ground is emptiness), and the Logos (where the ground is change and dynamism).

If we look at it from the other direction, starting with true nature, we see the spiritual universe manifesting in five boundless dimensions, which then differentiate into diamond vehicles, each one providing information about true nature. The essential aspects are then a further differentiation of true nature, revealing its various qualities and their particular characteristics. And then finally we come to the soul and then to the ego self. So to orient ourselves in this bigger picture, we need to understand how the ego relates to the soul and to all the various aspects, diamond vehicles, and boundless dimensions. We also need to appreciate how the living soul, freed from the structuring of ego, relates to the aspects, diamond vehicles, and boundless dimensions.

For a real understanding of all of this to take place, it is important to find a way to see it all for yourself, to discover and understand your own relationship to each element experientially. And in the Diamond Approach, we use, amongst other things, the psychological tool of object relations to help with that. Object relations refers to the recognition that it is through one's earliest relationships with others that the basic impression of oneself (the perceived "subject" in the relationship) is formed and that this is dependent on whatever impression one has formed of the other person (the perceived "object" of the relationship). The internalized memory of these early object relations is rarely a true reflection of the actual relationship. Nevertheless, the resulting fixed impressions of self and other plus the emotional charge felt in the relationship between them (love, desire, frustration, etc.) are carried over into all subsequent relationships, acting as a filter through which they are experienced.

Our early object relations affect how we view ourselves and anything that feels other than us, so we can look at and explore all the images and reactions that our history has left us with and see how they shape our relationship to our living consciousness or soul. Studying the historical content that shapes our experience will also reveal the relationship of that content to the various aspects, diamond vehicles, and boundless dimensions. Those relationships are not just "psychological" in the way that we normally understand that term—that is, something that pertains only to the mind. The medium of our soul has a substantiality to it, and the impact of our object relations leaves its mark on this impressionable substance of consciousness. In fact, the ego is nothing but the soul structured by the images of those object relations and all the other impressions from our past. Hence, the inner reality of the soul—our inner subjective experience, with its feelings, thoughts, sensations, and images—is all patterned by these historical impressions. Even our ordinary perception of the physical universe is influenced by this inner patterning of our subjectivity.

The main method used to gain an experiential understanding of everything is inquiry. This is the practice of observing and exploring our own felt experience in the moment, allowing it to be whatever it is and being open and curious to see what is true in it. We also look at how that truth is veiled, distorted, and shaped by object relations, projections, and identifications from the past. Most of the time, inquiry is oriented toward our own personal process in a way that will reveal the aspects, vehicles, and dimensions in our own soul. Here, however, we're continuing our inquiry in a way that isn't so focused on understanding our individual experience. It is inquiry into true nature as ground, the nature of reality itself, and how that relates to our soul, our ego, and everyday life.

In pursuing this inquiry into the deeper dimensions of true nature, the process will not always be synchronized with your own personal inquiry or unfoldment. For instance, a reaction to what I'm introducing at any point might be, "Fine, but how is this relevant to me? In my process I'm dealing with such and such, and I can't see how this will help me where I am now." That might be true on one level. But even if it's not directly related to what's going on with you right now and concerns a dimension of experience that seems far away from your understanding, by inquiring into it you may recognize by way of contrast more about where you are at the moment.

You see, the way consciousness works is that when a deeper consciousness meets a more superficial consciousness, they will always come toward an equilibrium. This means that if two people get together and one of them has a brighter and more intense light than the other, after a while their levels of light will converge. So I might introduce something that makes you feel, "Well, this isn't relevant to me—it's way beyond my level of understanding and consciousness." But if you work with it, if you try to understand it, it's bound to affect you in a way that leaves your light closer to that more brilliant light. The things I'm introducing here may not be completely understandable, relevant, or approachable for each individual. But every single person can benefit from them; it's just that each person will benefit differently, to a different degree.

This inquiry into the deeper dimensions is the focus of the teaching we're working with now, and it is perhaps a different realm from the usual content of your personal inquiry. Your personal inquiry will now include how you are impacted by this exploration of divine love, whether it feels relevant to you in the moment or not. After all, your inquiry has to be open to everything in your life, especially what's happening now, right? I mean, if you decide you only want to inquire into things that relate to what's going on inside you, what about the rest of your life? What happens if you fall in love, or somebody falls in love with you? Do you say, "No, sorry, that's not a proper inquiry, I'm not going to look into that"? Or if somebody robs your house, do you say, "No, that isn't relevant to my inquiry, so I'm not going to inquire into it"? Life is always dealing you impacts, one after the other. And this teaching is what is impacting you now. The teaching is providing you with its own impacts to be inquired into.

Inquiry may at first seem obvious and fairly simple—you just talk about your experience and try to understand what is going on, right? However, inquiry is much more than that. It is actually a refined spiritual practice. And though you may feel you get the hang of what it is by doing it for a while, it is not in fact a "doing" but a practice of nondoing. Inquiry cannot be fully understood until you understand all the dimensions of your spiritual nature. Every time you come to understand another aspect or another dimension, you understand inquiry in a deeper way, and the practice becomes more precise, more powerful. You come to see that the practice of inquiry is an expression of the whole teaching, not just one particular part of it.

However, when people have just begun the work, all they really know is their body, their personality, and their life situation. Therefore, for a few years they're bound to be mainly inquiring into and working on various life issues and emotional states, which usually involves a lot of pain and suffering as they uncover and work with all the object relations, identifications, and suffering from their past. That's what arises first as you inquire into your inner experience. And then as you go deeper, you discover that you are an actual organism of consciousness—a soul—that thinks, feels, acts, and is present. And you realize that your ego or personality—with all its habitual thoughts and reactions—is just a conditioned and limited manifestation of that soul.

As you feel the limitations of the structure that is your ego or personality, you recognize the "holes" in it—the parts of your soul where you have lost touch with your true nature. By becoming aware of the ways we avoid or cover these holes in our consciousness, we begin to recognize what has been lost, and the aspects of true nature that are inherent in our soul become accessible once more. You discover that your living consciousness has particular spiritual flavors, which are the essential aspects: compassion, strength, will, peace, joy, clarity, and many others. For many people there is then a long phase where there is a duality in their experience, a fluctuation between the familiar activity of the personality and the increasing emergence of spiritual qualities. Over time it becomes clear how the two are qualitatively different—the aspects are characterized by an immediacy of presence and knowing, which is lacking in our ego life.

As we become serious about understanding the totality of ourselves—in terms of our personality and essence—we recognize that we need to come to an understanding of our essential nature as it lives in the depth of our personal experience. And we cannot completely know our depth if we don't understand the relationship of the aspects to the boundless dimensions. That's because we can't really understand our true nature when we just experience love inside our heart, or strength in our belly, or intelligence in our head. That's not the whole story. Yes, we may be experiencing our true nature, but we're still experiencing it from the perspective of the personality. It's still from the perspective of the ego, a separate individuality.

Even though this dualistic realm is useful in many ways, and we always start from it, it is not sufficient for our understanding of reality to be complete. Even though spiritual experience and illumination can occur in this realm of experience, it is limited on its own, and the soul needs to transition to other realms, such as the boundless nondual dimensions of reality. There are limitations to how much of our true nature we can see in the dualistic world because it is being filtered through psychic structures that are not real, and the ego cannot see this because it is one of those structures. When we confront and penetrate these basic structures, the essential aspects reveal themselves as not being bounded by our body. They are not bounded by our physical extent or by our physical location, and this reveals our true nature as boundless—pervasive and infinite, extending everywhere.

As we've noted, the boundless dimension that we're focusing on now, Divine Love, is usually the first one that arises and is the easiest and most accessible. As we explore this dimension, we can see how it reveals most directly the relationship between the aspects and reality as a whole, or ultimate Being. It's the relationship between the spiritual qualities of the individual soul and divinity.

We can then begin to appreciate that the aspects, those spiritual qualities that human beings have such as compassion and love, true will and strength, are what make us human, and this is precisely because they are divine qualities. They are differentiations out of the nature of the universe, or the nature of God. What makes us human is that our depth has a divinity to it, something that is normally seen as beyond the human. I'm always surprised if someone tells me they are experiencing something very deep, such as deep spaciousness, boundless love, or beingness, and then says that this state makes them feel they are no longer human. I always wonder what "human" means to that person. People often think that what makes them human is their anger, jealousy, or weakness, but what really makes us human are our essential qualities, even if these qualities are not part of most people's conventional experience.

Over time, as we gradually reconnect to all the various essential aspects, they can develop and come to have a diamond-like quality—a sense of clarity and precision that reveals distinct knowledge and understanding with each aspect. This more precise understanding of our essential nature then begins to expose more of the underlying structure of our personality and its limitations—for instance, the limitation of the ahamkara, or the ego principle, which I discussed in chapter 2. And as we begin to see that, the structure becomes more transparent and our inner being gradually becomes more pervasive.

This usually involves dealing with fundamental structures and beliefs about who we are, the primary ones being our sense of identity and our sense of individuality. Identity is self-recognition. It's the answer to the question, "Who am I?" or "How do I know myself?" We usually respond, "Here I am. I am so and so and I am such and such." Individuality, on the other hand, is the sense of being an entity that extends in space and time, with distinct boundaries. The sense of individuality comes from this entity having an individual will, which enables it to make its own decisions. And it's the sense of identity that enables you to recognize that that entity is you and not somebody else; it gives it a characteristic flavor. These are the two basic structures that support our familiar experience of being a separate individual.

As we see through our identity and recognize that it is simply the sum of all the thought processes that have developed since childhood, we begin to experience who we are differently. We are no longer an individual experiencing essence; we are essence that has developed something that we call a personality. We see that what we are *is* essential nature, *is* presence, but that in our early development our soul needed to develop an identity based on the external world. And as we understand our sense of individuality—this feeling of entityhood that tells us that we are a unit in space and time—we recognize that it too is just a part of our ego development. It's not something we were born with, and it is not inherent in our soul.

We begin to experience then that our true identity, which is essential presence, is not just something here inside of us. It's not that you've got your presence over there, and I've got mine over here, and we're separate. Presence is not dispersed in small pieces throughout humanity; it is just one thing, and it's how we're all connected. All of humanity has the same essence, and we recognize that this essence is also the underlying nature of the whole of existence, of everything that manifests, of the whole world of appearance. Everything in the universe has this same nature. And when that is recognized, I move from talking about essence to talking about being. Essence is when I'm talking about the nature of the soul; being is when I'm talking about the nature of everything. In truth they are the same thing.

I said at the beginning of this teaching that it would involve a shift of focus from the experience of the individual soul to the experience of the whole of existence. And when we understand the connection of the soul to the larger perspective, it means that we understand what the boundless dimensions really mean, and that is when we begin to understand what spirituality truly means. We cannot understand spirituality if we don't understand divinity, if we don't understand the cosmic being or the nature of everything. If you only understand *yourself* as essential nature, you are only just beginning to know spirituality. To truly experience the spiritual or mystical is to experience the nature of everything, which is the same thing as the being of God. That is the work we are doing now.

We are not working just so that you feel your essence inside you and resolve your issues and that's it. That's what happens at the beginning—and we explored that in the first volume of this Journey of Spiritual Love series—but now we're concerned with the big picture, the whole story. Some teachings try to give you the whole story right from the beginning, but it's difficult to absorb, except in an intellectual way. In this work we want to learn experientially, little by little, so that you're gradually learning the teaching and at the same time learning what you yourself are and what reality is.

As your experience of the aspects and your essential nature is no longer felt to be something that is only inside you, you begin to see that you don't stop at your skin. Your soul doesn't stop at your skin, and neither does your essence. The only reason why your essence stops at your skin is because you think it does, because that's what you believe. The more you see through that belief, which is part of the ego principle, the more your essence expands, and it gets bigger and more expanded until you feel, "Oh, it's really big now!" When you feel so expanded, it can feel like you're filling the room, but although you're expanding, chances are you're still believing that you stop at your skin—it's just that your skin has gotten as big as the room. Only when you see through the skin as a boundary do you realize that you don't actually have a size or shape. You're everywhere. That's why we say "omnipresence"; you recognize your presence is now omnipresence because it really is everywhere.

What does it mean when I say your presence is everywhere? Well, it doesn't mean that you suddenly know what's happening in Rome or New Delhi. That's what many people understand by omnipresence, so of course it doesn't make sense to them. "Oh, it can't be true that I'm everywhere," they say, "because if I was, then I would know everything that's happening everywhere." No, that's not what I mean by omnipresence. What it means is that there's a *sense* that you're everywhere; that's how it feels. When you look out through your eyes, you see that your quality of being goes on infinitely, but that doesn't mean that you can see all the physical detail infinitely.

It's the same as with space. When you look around, you see and know that space holds everything and that space goes on forever, right? Well, your true nature goes on forever, just like space. And just as space is indivisible and has no beginning or end, so it is with true nature and infinite oneness. And by the way, it may be possible for someone with deep realization of oneness to be able to see what is happening in Rome or New Delhi. It's not impossible, but it's not basic to what we are exploring here. And anyway, it's not the point; the point is to be free from the limitation of our identity and our sense of boundary.

As we lose our boundaries, we recognize that there is only this boundless, infinite atmosphere and that all the essential qualities are basically differentiations and condensations of that atmosphere. We see that the atmosphere condenses into dense drops, and these drops are our souls, and the whole physical universe is formed out of densification and condensation of that atmosphere, all swimming within the ocean of it.

Of course, this perspective of the whole universe being pervaded by this reality, from which everything is formed and in which everything swims, doesn't accord with the scientific perspective of things. So if you're thinking scientifically, you'll have trouble with this perspective. This is because our modern Western science is inherently physically reductionistic. And more than that, it takes duality to be the true condition of reality. If you're thinking that way, why not put your scientific mind on the shelf for now? Not forever, because it's good to bring it back again when you've experienced this boundless reality. Then you can see how the two perspectives interrelate, which they do—there's no antithesis between them.

The spiritual perspective can hold the scientific perspective easily, no problem, with no contradiction. However, the scientific perspective cannot hold the spiritual one, at least not the scientific perspective as we have it now. That's why if you're a spiritual person, you can't argue with somebody who's taking the rational scientific perspective. They have to leave their scientific universe for a while in order to get the spiritual perspective, because the scientific perspective cannot hold spirit; in fact, it excludes spirit.

What we notice about this boundless atmosphere or ocean is its direct presence, its thereness. It is a palpable, substantial presence that you can sense physically. There's a hereness, an "I-am-ness" to it, but it's not just the I-am-ness of your own individual presence; this is the whole universe saying "I am." It is being, it is essence, it is presence; and this presence is consciousness at the same time. It is a shoreless ocean of consciousness, and you can feel how every single atom of it is consciousness itself. I don't mean consciousness in the sense of being conscious of other things, the way our mind can be conscious of chairs and trees and things. It is conscious in the sense that it's conscious or aware of its *own* existence. It is a conscious presence. So when you feel yourself in this boundless dimension, you feel your existence everywhere. Again, that doesn't necessarily mean that you see with your eyes the forms that existence is taking everywhere; you just feel the boundless existence itself as a conscious presence. You are conscious of the being of everything, an indivisible medium of being, conscious of itself. And you feel infinite.

I described in chapter 1 how this conscious presence is also light, a glowing radiance that is like the very substance of light, as if it's made up of an ocean of photons, but not physical ones—they're photons of a more spiritual kind. We know that light is fundamental to existence, and what we're seeing now is that light in the physical universe is only one manifestation of this inner light. The nature of this boundless consciousness is light and radiant while also light in the sense of weightless. It is illuminated and without heaviness and yet experienced as a fullness and a hereness. Its presence is unmistakable. What we also recognize is that although this presence has no weight, it has a flavor, a taste, and a texture. Its texture is a softness, an incredibly delicate softness, like a baby's skin. It's like the most delicate powder, almost like fluffy clouds, but clouds that are warm and not wet. This delicate soft texture can be both felt and tasted as sweet. It's an exquisite kind of sweetness.

That's the reason I call it love, because it's so sweet and soft. That's how people think of love, as something sweet and soft, right? And as I said before, I call it divine partly because of its purity, its sense of being fresh and newly created, but also because it is everywhere and everything is made out of it. It's like the whole world, the whole universe, is sculpted from glowing cotton candy or candy floss. When you're experiencing the world in the dimension of Divine Love, everything glows from within; the walls glow, the air glows, everybody glows with an inner light. And the delicate softness and sweetness of it feels like it melts you, it makes you surrender, and it makes you let go.

But what does it mean when we describe this process as one of letting go, of surrender? It means that as you feel this boundless presence, it begins to expose the truth that you are of its nature. We call that surrender, as you lose your sense of separateness. We call it melting, but all that's melting are your ideas, your beliefs, about who you think you are. So you think you're a physical body, and then you realize you're soft and malleable. You're light—you're made out of light and love. So you might say, "Oh, the light melted me," but as we've seen, it's just a figure of speech, a notion that doesn't really describe what is happening. All that's happening is that you're discovering who and what you are.

As you abide in this state, the presence you feel has a sense of grace to it that is twofold. There is grace in the sense that you perceive everything to be graceful, beautiful, and harmonious, and you can *feel* this grace, its sensation and texture. And there is also grace in the sense that this state feels like a blessing. It's a blessing to know this purity and divinity and to see that the whole universe is blessed. But it's not only that the whole universe is blessed; it's also that the whole universe is nothing but blessings made out of this grace. So it's graceful, you see, and graced at the same time.

PRACTICE SESSION
THE JOURNEY TOWARD BOUNDLESS LOVE
· · ·

In this chapter we have explored the larger context of the Diamond Approach path and how this spiritual journey leads to an exploration of the boundless dimensions and in particular, the dimension of Divine Love. Now would be a good time for you to inquire into how you are impacted by this process. You have been invited to go deeper into your experience of yourself, into what feels true and real, and we've seen that exploring your own inner experience can challenge ideas about being a separate entity. This can ultimately lead to experiencing a pervasive ground of presence and, in this case, one of radiance, lightness, softness, and sweetness.

As in the previous chapter, you will be doing a monologue, working with one or two other people if possible. Each person in turn will take fifteen minutes to inquire into what has been stirred up by reading about this journey toward boundless love. If you are on your own you can take fifteen minutes to write out your inquiry. Consider the following questions:

What resonates with you in what you have read?
Do you notice being inspired or opened or awakened to
    expanded possibilities in your own experience? Or do

you feel reactions or resistance to these ideas, focusing on ways they don't feel relevant for you?

Are you attracted to or turned off by things that were said in this chapter?

What do you notice going on in your body as you do your inquiry?

Let your inquiry take you wherever it wants as you discover where you are in this process.

· · · · ·

FOUR

The Body of Light

Each boundless dimension has what I call a diamond issue, a particular barrier or obstacle to realizing that dimension. In fact each dimension has many such issues, but there's usually one particular one that opens the door to that dimension. We can identify these diamond issues by recognizing the main structures in our soul that are blocking our experience of that dimension. With Divine Love we've already seen that the structure that cuts us off from it is that of the separate self with its two facets: identity and entityhood. So this is the diamond issue. In order to understand how this issue is connected with this boundless dimension, we draw on our psychological understanding. We ask: How did our structure of separate individuality develop—the structure of being a unit in space and time?

There are many psychological theories that deal with this question. One of the best I know is Margaret Mahler's. It says that the sense of identity—and its associated sense of being a separate entity—emerges from infancy through the development of certain images and impressions of what you are. These impressions are initially based on what she calls the body image, which forms the first building block of identity. What the infant experiences within their body—their inner atmosphere—is what gives them in time their sense of self-recognition or identity. In contrast, the physical impressions that result from contact with the outside reveal the shape, contours, and size of their body, resulting in the infant's sense of being a separate entity. So the sense of self-recognition as an entity with identity—which is what it means to be an individual—is based originally on the body. In other words, who we take ourselves to be, the ahamkara, or ego principle, is primarily based on identifications with the body, both inner and outer. If you take your body to be you, then you believe you are a unit in space and time.

So the fundamental diamond issue here is the identity with the body. Everybody has it; all egos have it. The personality identifies with the body more than anything else; it believes the body to be the most fundamental aspect of what it is. Everybody believes they are basically a body that has feelings and thoughts. That's why you say, "I have a mother and a father, and I was born on such-and-such a date." When you say, "I'm celebrating my birthday," what are you celebrating? It's your body's birthday—what else? Your soul wasn't born at that time. Your nature wasn't born at that time. That's why I don't care about birthdays, and everybody thinks I'm weird. To keep celebrating my body's birth every year just reinforces a belief that that's who I am. Every year everybody gives you gifts and celebrates who you are, but what that really means is you are considered to be your body.

And when you say, "That's my mother and father," what does that mean? Who are they the mother and father of? Just your body. When you know your true nature, you recognize that your true parent is the divine being. You are a child of divinity; you always have been, and you always will be. It's true that your body has a physical mother and father, and your soul has been somewhat influenced by those parents. But your soul probably began a long time before them and will go on after them.

So we can see the depth and pervasiveness of our ubiquitous identification with the body. It is actually scientifically reinforced, for it is so far the view of our Western science that the body is paramount, and it is actually the source of consciousness. This is the exact opposite of Aristotle, and all spiritual teachings. It's a culturally reinforced identification, but it's also a natural identification for us to develop from the outset. As soon as we are born we have to learn how to operate in the world that our parents and society see as physical, and we do that through the vehicle of our body. And, of course, we soon come to believe that we are this vehicle. Now, I'm not saying that our soul and our body are two completely discontinuous things. What I am saying is that the body is just a surface phenomenon of the soul, and that we have a tendency to see the surface of something and take it to be the whole thing. In ancient times, people didn't know they had hearts, lungs, and intestines. They thought that they were just skin and that it was probably solid all the way through; they imagined their bodies were just a thick tube of skin. Unless someone saw the inside of a dead person, they didn't know any different. So even though we now know more about the inner reality of our bodies, when you take your body to be you, you are missing your own deeper inner reality; you are taking the surface of your being to be you. And you don't realize that this surface can be shed, just like a snake's skin can be shed. This is actually what happens at the time of death.

There is then this very deep, very entrenched and crystallized belief that I am my body. If something happens to my body, it happens to me. So even when we experience our spiritual essence, this identity with the body makes it very difficult for us to recognize that this essence is actually who and what I am. It also makes it difficult to see that what I really am is not confined within the boundary of this body. If we believe that our body defines who we are, and our body ends at our skin, then we believe that all of what we are ends at our skin, that our consciousness or soul ends at our skin.

It's no simple thing to recognize this identity with the body and see through it. Just saying, "Oh yeah, I can see that I really believe I am my body," does not mean you've seen the identification. You have to look very deep, because there are many levels of identification and the important ones are so deep that they are completely unconscious and implicit. That's where you believe so much that the body is you that you'll instinctively fight for it. Don't you believe deep down that your existence depends on the life of your body? That's why people are so afraid of death—we know the body definitely ceases to exist then, so if I believe I am my body, well, that's it for me. Many of our difficulties in life are a result of this powerful identification with the body. And I'll emphasize again: I'm not saying that the body isn't a part of us, or that it's something bad. I'm just stating the fact that our core—our essential true nature—is not the body. The body is simply a form, an external form that our true nature takes. And true nature actually needs the body to live on Earth as a human being.

When you truly see this identity and how much you believe that you are the body, you see how that limits your experience of what you are, and you can then recognize not only that you are essential nature but also that this essential nature doesn't have to have a physical form. It doesn't have to be bounded by the form of the body. And that's when you really start to experience boundlessness. Seeing through your identity with the body is key to seeing through the issues of identity and individuality and recognizing boundlessness.

It's a process that goes through several transitions or stages, and its progress will depend on how identified we are with the body at all the different levels of that identity. When we first experience divine love, as love or light, we may experience it as something that is inside our body. We may be experiencing boundlessness, but we are *somebody* who is experiencing it, so we're still identifying with the body. That is how most people experience boundlessness; they might say, "Oh yes, there is light; I see light everywhere." That's good, that's the beginning, but it's just the first step, and it's not what I mean when I talk about experiencing boundlessness.

As you see through your identity with your body more and more, you become the light itself. You recognize, "I am this light." And that's the first stage of being a transcendent witness. Although you are aware of your body, you recognize that you are the light, and not the body. I'll tell you about my own experience of this with a few lines from my journal:

> Evening, on a walk. Being the divine light, I experience myself as a very light awareness, but as a witness. I am actually not identified with the body. I am aware of the body walking. Being the divine light is really a transcendence of everything.

So in this experience I am this light; I know I am the light, and I can see my body walking. It's as if someone's hovering up above the body and seeing it. But actually I wasn't hovering; it's more that somehow I was everywhere, and I was seeing the body walking along the road. And that's the beginning of being the light, being divine love.

The next step is to recognize that you are this divine love and light and that it pervades everything, including the body. So divine love contains the body; it holds it. It's like the body sits in this light that I am, and that is different from the earlier experience where the light seemed to be inside the body; now the body is in the light. And then you recognize that this light or divine love that you are, which includes your body, is just part of the divine love that is the nature of everything. Everything is divine love, and you are part of it. This means you are part of God, a cell in a cosmic body. This is a nondual experience, but not one that's emphasized by many of the nondual teachings. It is useful for living a personal life from a nondual perspective, however.

After that comes the experience of being divinity itself. It is the awareness that I am this love, this consciousness, this presence, and I am everything, not just a part of everything. At this point there is complete identity with the wholeness and oneness of everything. The body is just one of the things that constitute me, and I am far more than that. I am everybody and everything; I am the walls and the doors, the mountains, the skies, and the stars. I am also the very nature of all these things—that's how I am them. I know myself as the true nature of everything.

The next step, which is the most difficult one, is to recognize what the body is. Basically, you see that you are the divinity, and you are also a particular condensation out of it. And that condensation becomes a body of light. You recognize that the body itself is light; it is this divine love but in a particular form. So we can see that at the beginning, when we are identified with the body, we are not even identified with the true body. We're identified with an image we've developed of what the body is. We don't even know what the real body is. When we're free of that mental construct, that story we developed about the body, we can begin to experience what the body truly is—a body of light. Because when you know that everything is light, you recognize that even your body is light.

It's very difficult for people to develop an awareness of this because our familiar experience of the body is so physical. I mean, your body hurts, right? And we can say from the scientific point of view that the pain is real. Well, it's true, sometimes the body hurts. But who says a body of light can't hurt? The body of light is pure awareness, and when it hurts it's due to an intensification of sensation in that field of awareness. The other way we can experience such an intensification of sensation is through pleasure.

Now, when we recognize that the body is a body of light, that isn't necessarily the same thing as what people sometimes mean when they refer to a body of light *inside* the physical body. That is a specific development of the soul, which does happen, but it's a more limited experience where you're still subject to the duality between the physical and the divine.

So the first level of experiencing the light is you *experiencing* the light, but the real experience is when you know that you *are* the light, you *are* the love. However, the fullest experience is to recognize that everything is that light and love, not just the individual you.

PRACTICE SESSION
IDENTIFICATION WITH THE BODY
• • •

It's time to explore what has been discussed. We know now that identification with the body is the diamond issue that has to be worked through to know boundlessness, and it's an issue for everybody, so we'll explore it in the form of two repeating questions. As in the "Ownership of Experience" practice in chapter 1, each person will answer each of the following questions for fifteen minutes. If you are on your own, you can write out your answers for fifteen minutes.

Why is it important to identify with your body?

There are many reasons you believe your body is fundamental to your identity, to who you are. This is a chance to explore what comes up spontaneously when you consider this fundamental identification.

Tell me a way you are identifying with your body.

Look at the ways in present time that you identify with your body at different levels: by picturing it, thinking about it, feeling it, or any other of the many different ways of relating to it.

• • • • •

Questions and Comments

Student: I have many questions, but I think they all come down to one really: What constitutes existence?

A. H. Almaas: Well, first of all, existence is one of the essential aspects. It is inherent to all manifestations of true nature, all aspects and dimensions. And presence is simply the sense of existing in a palpable immediate way. When you experience the aspect of existence, you feel your existence and also the existence of the world. You know what existence is as an actual feeling, an actual state. If the question then is, *What exists?* that's what you see in the boundless dimensions. The boundless dimensions bring the experience of what reality is, which means what truly exists. Everything that ordinarily exists still exists there in fact, but it doesn't exist in the same way. So actually the question isn't, *What exists?* but rather *What is the mode of existence?* as that changes depending on the dimension. In the dimension of Divine Love, as we've seen, the mode of existence is one of light, love, and presence.

S: So is there any way of talking about me being there in this existence?

AH: You being there?

S: Yeah. Me.

AH: The you that you usually know yourself as can't exist there. Your mode of existence would change. When you exist in the dimension of Divine Love, your form exists, and the body is still there, but your recognition of yourself is different. The you that you're used to feeling won't be there. It will be something different, and how things exist will also be different. For instance, you won't exist as something separate from other things. In the boundless dimensions there are no separate objects. It's just like it is in your dreams. When you dream, you dream of yourself, your partner, your house, your dog—your dreams are filled with other people and things, right? And they all feel real in the dream, as if they exist as separate entities. But do they really exist separately from each other? No, because it's all in your mind, isn't it? Well, the whole universe is in God's mind—it's the same thing.

S: A question that arose for me was, "Can I be fully in my body? Can I fully have my experience and enjoy my body, take responsibility and care for it and all that, and not identify with it at all?" So I wondered, "What exactly is 'identification'"? It seemed to me that maybe it's like a contraction or a kind of fixation, either an ideation or some kind of physical sensation that gets stuck and held on to. So it's no longer a flowing process but kind of a fixation, either mental, physical, or emotional. It's stuck.

AH: It's true, yes. The identification with the body, just like any other identification, is a fixation, a contraction, a holding on. And often someone says, "To have my body I have to hold on to it, right?" Which isn't true. The truth is that without the identification with the body you'll be more relaxed, and you'll be more aware of what's going on in the body. And because of that, you can take care of it even more effectively.

S: So the identification with the body . . . that doesn't have to be there for me to experience or sense things?

AH: No. It actually limits your ability to experience. Identification with the body brings in the structure of the self that is identified with the body. There is a network of tension patterns that goes along with this ego structure and makes the body more opaque and tense instead of open and supple.

S: So the identification is a way that I limit myself, a way that I fixate and contract myself, and hold that in some way in order to get a sense of identity. And that's false because I already exist.

AH: Yes. The point of identity is to have an identity, a way or a feeling of self-recognition, regardless of whether it makes us feel the body more or less. Many people have an identification with their body that results in them not feeling their body at all. They believe they are their body, but they don't feel much there. And in fact the less they identify with it, the more they relax in terms of their identity, the more they actually feel the body and its juices and fullness. But that's one question that arises, definitely: "If I don't have this identity with the body, what will happen? Can I take care of it, or will I just forget about it?" Well, you won't forget about it, definitely not. It's just like with your clothes. You may be attached to your clothes, but you don't usually identify with them, and yet you still wash them regularly and take care of them. It's even more the case with the body, because your body is always there, not like your clothes. And if you recognize the true nature of your body, then you see it is made out of love, and then of course you love it too and take care of it. After all, it is the vehicle by which you can experience everything, so it is of enormous value to you.

S: There does seem to be a special connection with it.

AH: I would certainly say it's special.

S: I mean, I can't get another one at the Gap.

AH: Not in this lifetime, you can't. Who knows, in a hundred years or two, maybe you could get another one. In the age of the cyborgs.

S: I saw something I've never seen before about this identification, which is the value of it. If I inquire into it, I see that it draws out and makes available to divine love everything that is needing it in my system. I've been very preoccupied with the physical layer recently, selling my house and trying to find a new one and concerned about bringing my mother into this new situation. So my body has been having a lot of stress and difficulty. And when I was going into the identification with the body, my first response was, "Oh, there's nothing right about identifying with it." And then, as I inquired into the state of the body and felt the empty shell of the structure of ego identity, I discovered that the vulnerability of the needs that I had been suppressing became apparent. And then melting started happening, and the presence of love was there for the condition of vulnerability and the need for attention of the parts of myself that find it intolerable to be doing all this grown-up activity. So, identification has its own brilliancy. But my first response to it was, "It's not the truth, so it must be wrong." But it has a function.

AH: Yes, it's true. Identification has a function. It's a way for being to embody, to be in the body. It's a way to come into this world, and part of that process is to identify with the body. It's part of the process of ego development, but that's only a stage, you see. However, we get stuck in one stage, and then we think that's the whole story. That's the difficulty.

S: But the stuckness moved when I became aware of the vulnerability that the body was expressing by holding itself in tension, which I wasn't taking into account.

AH: So as you became conscious of that identification, it dissolved—you disidentified. The identification dissolves, but the body is still there, and you can continue to operate with it in the physical world. You operate more effectively then because you're not as scared. You're not scared of dying as much, so it gives you more courage to operate in the world. The vulnerability you are experiencing is most likely due to the body relaxing and revealing the identity structure and its history, which has lots of needs and vulnerability.

S: Could you say something about the relationship with physical death? I'm quite confused about what you said: "It's only my body's birthday" and "I didn't begin, and I won't end." I'm not sure whether you mean that divine love exists forever and an eternity, and this immediate form will be dissolved or reabsorbed into it, so you'll be fully in divine love and no longer a condensation of it. Or whether you have some experience that the soul exists apart from the body, so that individuality or condensation will continue to exist.

AH: After death, is that what you're asking?

S: After physical death. And before death, physical birth.

AH: Yes, the soul can exist apart from the physical body. That's definitely true. However, at the same time, when your identity is in the dimension of Divine Love, if you recognize your true nature, that you are the same consciousness that is the nature of everything, then the concept of death breaks down altogether. Because what could die, then? If you are everything, then you can't die. It doesn't make sense that you're born or you die.

S: Well, in the sense that the soul is a condensation out of that, the soul could die if it was dispersed.

AH: Yes, the soul can die. But as divine love, you are bigger than the soul.

S: Right. But you are also saying that the soul . . .

AH: That on the level of the soul, yes, it can survive the physical body. So when I say that you were not born at your birth, I was referring to the soul but also to divine love. As a soul, that's right, you weren't born then. We could at least say that you were born at or around the time of conception, if you don't believe in life before conception. But from the boundless perspective of divine love, well, the whole idea of time changes, you see. Because you think of the body in terms of movement and time, so it has a birth and death. But from the perspective of this unity of consciousness, there is no such thing. So yes, the soul is there before the body and after the body.

Remember that the soul relieves itself of the ego structure, which gives it identity based on the body. When the ego identity is gone, the body remains as an expression of the boundless consciousness of love. It no longer defines the soul but is simply part of it. We can feel the soul dissolving, but it is momentary; it always returns, for the soul is the expression of consciousness that allows consciousness to have conscious experience. The soul is the organ of experience and there is no experience without a soul—an individual conscious being. But here the soul is a conscious being that is free of ego structuring and patterns, including identity with the body. So if there is experience after death it obviously needs the vehicle or lens of the soul to have experience or be aware of consciousness.

S: Okay. And, like the other person, I was struggling with this question that if I was disidentified from the body, then I thought of that in terms of being like, dissociated. There are times I've felt dissociated, where I'm really not connected with my body. And so I thought in terms of, "Well, I wouldn't care about taking care of it. Why would I even be motivated to have a body if I felt myself to be divine love?" So can you say a bit more about how you would love your body, because it is love?

AH: Yes. You see, you can be divine love in the state of just witnessing the body but not being the body. And that can be dissociation. Some people can go to the boundless or nondual dimension of experience through dissociation, as when they are going away from a trauma. This is possible, but it does not bring the liberation from the patterning influence and suffering of the trauma. However, with the other states I mentioned, when the body is part of everything and you are everything, it's not the same as dissociation, because you're feeling the body much more intensely and completely then.

S: And you're feeling deeply connected with it.

AH: Oh yes. It's like the body itself is pure consciousness then. So you can't call that dissociation because dissociation is a lessening of consciousness.

S: I find that when I look at my identification, it's not with the physical body itself but with my thoughts and feelings and sensations and desires and hopes and all that. And when I look into that, it seems that it's still . . . , it's certainly from a point of duality and certainly stemming from my body and all about my body, but it's not of my body. And even when I think about essential states, it's still from that viewpoint. You know, like what does it do for me and for the states that I'll experience within my body. And that seems to be where I get stuck.

AH: Yes. So when you're identified with the body, that's how you operate. You tend to value the reality that contains your identity. So if your identity is in the physical body, then what has value is the physical universe. If your identity is with essence, then what's valuable is essential nature. If your identity is in divine love, you recognize that the divine experience is what's valuable. And, of course, the more of yourself that you include, the more objective your sense of value is. If you're only identified with the physical body, then you're taking only one layer of who you are and saying that's what's valuable. But from the perspective of divine love, you recognize the value of essence. And its value has nothing to do with what it gives you. At first we think the value of essence is that it gives me release, it gives me fulfillment, it gives me love, compassion, warmth, holding. All wonderful stuff, right? But when you break through to the level of boundless love or light, you realize that no, that's not the real value of essence. The real value of essence is simply that it is there. Because it is what is true, it is what is real.

And remember, when I say that our identity is not the body, I'm not devaluing the body in any way. The body is in some sense a dimension of presence, a dimension of presence that's necessary for us to be aware of all the dimensions of presence in this world. So that is its value. Without it, we couldn't actually have all this experience. And when I say our identity is divine love, beyond the soul, I'm not devaluing the soul. Because without the soul we wouldn't be able to experience divine love.

S: I had, and have, a lot of enthusiasm and joy and energy around this exercise. Because a theme came up that still remains. And it was the idea that with this whole thing about body identification comes the sense that I am here, and that's all that counts. There were a lot of new things that came up in the exercise, but from beginning to end I kept hearing it: "I am here." It's really charged, and it's great.

AH: Yes. Sounds wonderful. When you're experiencing your presence, that's the sense that I'm here. This "I am here," which is the presence of who you are, then exists on many levels, you see. Divine love is just one of the levels. When you feel "I am here, but I'm also everywhere," it includes "I am here." Because everywhere is also here and now.

S: For me, this exercise gave a new meaning to the line about the eyes being the window to the soul. I've realized recently that the way I can really have this experience of boundarylessness is through eye contact, which I never allowed myself before. And not just boundarylessness, but intimacy and expansiveness, and I can forget about my body. I can become "other" oriented, and it's a way I can connect with somebody else. I try to do that sometimes in the mirror, where I look into my own eyes to see if it will also take me away from myself. But it's a very different experience; it feels egotistical and limiting and I don't expand. I feel very contained and limited. So why can't I do it when I look in the mirror? Why can't I expand when I make eye contact with myself, like I can when I make eye contact with others?

AH: Interesting question. Because of divine love. As I said before, the desire, the tendency to seek contact, sharing, merging, communication, and love, all that expresses the fact that we are one in some dimension. So if you're looking into somebody's eyes, you're seeing yourself, in some sense. It's the same identity. It's easier to see that looking into somebody's eyes than looking in the mirror, because the light seems brighter there, in someone else. As for the eyes being a window into the soul, let's say that the body is a window into the soul. And the soul is a window into our true nature. And true nature is a window into divine being.

S: I take it that when you say we need a body to experience any of the dimensions, you mean we need the sensory apparatus. So how does the soul experience them when it's not coexistent with the body?

AH: You mean without the body, like after death?

S: Yeah. Without the sensory apparatus, how is there experience?

AH: I don't know exactly for sure, right? But you know you can have subtle perceptions. That you can see and hear things, but not through the physical body? When somebody can "see" their inner state, inside, they're not using their physical vision.

S: If I have an experience like that, however subtle it is, it always seems to me there's some aspect of my sensory apparatus involved. Is that not so?

AH: No. If you think about it, you'll see that isn't so. Your eyes don't look inside you. If you're actually seeing colors and shapes inside you, how are you seeing them? That's one example. And the other example is of course the well-known phenomenon of ESP.

S: I can only think that if I have such an experience, where I'm seeing colors inside, that somehow the way I'm perceiving it is connected to the fact that I have a body. It has something to do with knowing what it's like to have sensory apparatus.

AH: That's what you assume. But from the perspective of divine love you recognize that the body is not as fundamental as presence. As long as you identify with the body, the body seems to be the fundamental ground, and everything else happens to it or from it. But when you are on deeper ground, when you're seeing on the level of Divine Love or deeper dimensions like the Supreme dimension and the Absolute dimension, then your identity is in a place that holds the physical but is deeper than the physical. And then you realize that all consciousness comes from that deeper dimension. Not from the body. One way of seeing it is to imagine that the physical body perhaps adds more discrimination and differentiation to the soul than the soul can have on its own. However, while we are living physically and learning to realize ourselves physically, maybe our soul can develop a capacity for discrimination and experience that it didn't have before, which it can then use after the body is gone. So you then have the body of light that I talked about earlier. It's another body, a spiritual one.

FIVE

Complete Release

We've seen that when we explore the boundless dimensions, we're no longer just exploring the essence of the human being and of the soul, we're exploring the essence of reality, the essence of everything, the essence of the whole universe. And in exploring these dimensions, we begin to look more at where the essence we feel inside us comes from. Early in our journey we discover that we can experience different aspects of essence in our soul, which we refer to as, for example, red essence or strength, green essence or compassion, love, and will. But as we look beyond our own soul, the question arises, Where does it all come from?

As soon as you ask that question you begin to enter the boundless dimensions. That's because you soon recognize that essence doesn't come from inside you, say, from your liver or your intestines. But if you don't know about the boundless dimensions, how else are you going to see it and think of it? You're going to think it's probably all because of your hormones. When some people feel the flow of essence, they do actually think, "Oh, it's just the flow of my hormones or the flow of energy in my body." And so they never find out what is really there, what essence is, and where the qualities of it come from. But when you experience essence inside you, if you observe the unusual sense of its energy and presence, you recognize that it's obviously not a physical phenomenon. It doesn't feel physical, and yet it's still substantial. So you wonder, "What is it? And how come all this happens?" By exploring these questions, we discover the source of essence, where it comes from. And that's when we begin to open up, as the soul opens up to the boundlessness of essence. We recognize that it's not just inside us—it's everywhere.

And when I say that this boundless essence is everywhere and doesn't come from the body, remember this doesn't mean the body should be seen as something negative, something you need to reject or transcend. It's not like that. We've already seen that because this boundless love or presence is everywhere, it is the essence of everything. It's the nature of all physical reality, so that includes the body. If you've only experienced essence as something in your physical body, then you still don't know the true nature of the body—you're still thinking of your body biologically, and you don't know it spiritually yet. When you get to the boundless dimensions and see that your body is made out of your essence, and *everything* is made of essence, then you know that essence is not just something you feel inside your body. It's only the limitation of our understanding that makes us see essence as something that's inside us, or as something we haven't got inside us and need to get from someplace else.

So essence is here all the time. It's everywhere, and it's for everybody. This really is the best news possible. Some people say, "Well, I didn't know that before. Nobody told me, and I'm mad about that." Good, be mad. But the point of feeling and understanding your anger or hurt is to be able to connect to the truth that essence is here all the time. If you just continue to be angry, you'll just continue to separate yourself from it. If you continue to believe you're a separate, abandoned soul, well, you'll just stay separate from the ocean you live in. And then you'll keep on looking for it, searching for what's right under your nose.

That's why it's useful to see things from the perspective of the boundless dimensions. I teach about them because that's how I see things—I'm just describing the truth as I perceive it. It connects with some people though, and they say, "Yeah, that makes sense." Not only does it make sense, it also fulfills the heart, it releases the soul, and it cleanses the body. The body then becomes really juicy, open, and full, and we see that the body itself is made out of love and light.

So this is not like some teachings that say we should ignore the body and focus only on the spirit. What I'm saying is that by recognizing that your nature is more than physical and that you are not bound by your body, you open up to this other dimension, which still includes the body. Even if you identify with the body after that, you know that your body is not just physical anyway. And after a while you can't really identify with it any longer, not because you don't want to but because you can see that it's not a separate thing—it's made out of the same divine love and light as everything else.

And when we open up to this divine love, this nectar that composes the whole universe, we get a sense of its sweetness, its exquisiteness, and its harmony. Those are the qualities of the presence itself: sweetness, softness, a sense of flowing, a lightness, a radiance, and a glowing quality. And the effect it has on us is to bring a sense of release and freedom—complete release, complete freedom, and complete delight. There is a state of not having a care in the world. I mean, why would you have a care in the world if you realize that the whole world is love?

What's left then is to see the parts of you that don't see the omnipresent love and work through them. And that doesn't mean you question the love; you simply question those parts of you that don't see it—that's the intelligent thing to do. If you really feel this love for yourself, you'll begin to see all the places inside you that don't believe it's true. And so you ask, "What's all this about? Here it is, all this love, it's all around me. How come parts of me don't believe it?" Because if we really see the love and are convinced of it, if our mind accepts that, then the love will just be there. It doesn't matter then what suffering there is in you and in the world, because there is always freedom from it. There is always the possibility of liberation, delight, and a lightness of being. And if there is pain, the lightness can be felt as compassion. Where there's difficulty and barriers, the sense of freedom can become a source of strength and power. But it's a divine strength and a divine power, so it's much more potent and has a much greater impact.

I've talked about how the presence of divine love and its sweetness can manifest in us as a wanting of it, a yearning for it. It evokes a longing for merging and union. However, we can see now that there's another kind of longing that is closer to the truth of divine love—it's not just the wanting and yearning for union but a wanting and yearning for the freedom from care that this love brings. Because that is more what this state is: a condition of presence where there is no care, no conflict, no fear, no insecurity, and no need to worry about anything.

So the longing for a carefree condition reflects the longing for divine love. Below is an excerpt from my journal, from around the time I was learning about divine love. It will give you an idea of what can happen when this longing arises, one possible story of its unfolding.

Yesterday, I woke up feeling a deep sadness. Eyes full of tears. I do not know the cause of the sadness. In meditation, I start with the desire just to be aware. After a while I see the futility of it. I see that even paying attention is doing, is effort, and is based on desire. It's not always based on desire, but this time I am controlled by the desire to be free. I feel deep tears again. The sadness is connected with a longing and yearning for a completely free condition, where there is no need to even be aware. Where just being, by itself, is enough. I see and feel that I do not know what to do to reach such a state. I feel there is nothing I can do in this situation. Everything I do is effort, and effort does not work. Also, it's not what I want. I decide to not do anything. I don't want to keep making efforts. I want an effortless and completely carefree condition. If I always have to pay attention and be aware, then I am defeating myself. I give up trying. I give up practicing any technique, even awareness. I just let myself be there—whatever happens, happens.

I decide not to work on myself for a while. There's a constant feeling of irritation, frustration, and longing, as well as helplessness. As I feel the helplessness, it brings about a conscious light, which is love as well as light. It comes down through the head into the chest. It tastes slightly sweet and looks like a yellowish, golden-white liquid light. Obviously,

I am looking for the ease and release that this divine light can bring, where there is no contraction at all, no concerns whatsoever. Where the heart is open and happy and the mind is rested. This, then, leads to a discovery of the fundamental issue in all searching, even for enlightenment: the cycle of hope, desire, and rejection that blocks the flow of the love and light.

Understanding this dynamic of hope opens a big door that leads to an understanding of essence from an egoless perspective. After this realization, I experience the conscious light most of the time. I feel it in the chest, mostly in the subtle center at the sternum, which I call the mobius, in the form of merging gold light. Sometimes I see that I am feeling motivated by hope again, and with it comes comparison, rejection, suffering, and wanting release. But to my surprise, every once in a while a quiet voice, which seems to come from the mobius, says, "It's okay; it doesn't matter." And then there is no concern about changing anything or getting anywhere. There is only curiosity about the situation, without motivation.

As time passes, the conscious light becomes more present as I understand something about a kind of plastic boundary that I've become aware of around my body. I see that this boundary is the structure of being a limited individual. That's how the ego boundary becomes manifest, and here it feels to me as if it's made out of plastic—it has that kind of hard, resilient texture. And as I see this plastic boundary, I recognize what is preventing its dissolution: It is the hope for release and freedom from it. So I am approaching it with rejection and hope. Seeing that seems to melt the plastic into light, and so the boundary begins to dissolve.

A little while later, I am watching TV. At some point I become aware that I do not feel separate from the TV. Actually, what happens is I'm watching the TV, and suddenly I say, "God, it seems as if I'm there!" I remember it was a Western I was watching, and I said, "God, I am that Western! I am that cowboy!"

So it's curious, but that was for me the beginning of truly knowing boundlessness—I hadn't really known it very well before that. My journal continues:

As the subtle perception expands, the first thing I notice is that it is different from awareness without ego. In that experience there is no subject, only objects. Here, it's a different state. I do experience myself, as a presence that is some kind of conscious light. There are no boundaries to this sense of self—there is a subtle identity with everything. Looking out into the garden, I perceive that the garden is made of the same light that I am, and so I am the garden, I am the trees. The light is the foundation of everything; all objects spring from it and exist in it. Since the light is the origin and selfhood of everything, then I am aware that I am the light, and everything is in me, including the mind and body. I am aware of my identity with the sweet divine light by being it. I am all, I am everything. So when I look in the bedroom and see Marie, my wife, lying there sleeping, I recognize that she is also me, because she is the same sweet light. And as I recognize that, the light gets even sweeter. There is a subtle absence of all self-boundaries; it goes beyond the barrier of the individual experience. There is only one subject, and all objects are manifestations of that one subject. There is no duality; there is unity. The experience is shattering for the ego, but in a very quiet and subtle manner.

From this description of entering a boundless dimension, in this case Divine Love, you can see that it doesn't mean you should stop paying attention to physical reality. No, physical reality—the TV, the garden, the trees, my partner, my own body—it's all still there and needs to be attended to as usual. And there's no conflict in this, because we see that physical reality isn't separate from our essential nature, so it actually makes it easier for us to deal with the physical, not more difficult. So I'll say it once more: Entering the boundlessness doesn't mean rejecting the physical and not taking care of it. In fact we want to know our physical reality and our body as deeply as possible, and as we go deeper, we see what physical reality is rooted in, what holds it all, which awakens in our soul the longing for liberation and release.

So the approach of divine love can emerge in our soul as a longing for it, which can be felt as a longing for release and complete freedom from care and worry. Nevertheless, there may be barriers against feeling that longing for release. For instance, we might not think this release is really possible. We might have all kinds of doubts and worries about whether we could ever reach this carefree state, and say, "Well, what's the point in trying or even thinking about it?" We may feel so hopeless about it that we don't allow ourselves to even feel the longing for it. The problem then is that focusing on whether or not you will get what you long for cuts you off from the movement of your heart. You're not allowing the divine presence to touch you from within or to awaken in you the feeling of wanting to be closer to it.

PRACTICE SESSION
LONGING FOR RELEASE
· · ·

This exercise is an opportunity for you to explore the barriers to feeling the longing for release. It's done as a repeating question exercise like the ones in chapters 1 and 4. If you're practicing with other people, each person will have fifteen minutes to answer the following question. If you are practicing alone, you can write your response to yourself.

Tell me something that stops you from wanting complete release.

· · · · ·

Questions and Comments

Student: Traditionally some teachers, like Ramana Maharshi, say that for an enlightened person to be in the body is like trying to keep an elephant in the closet. You keep hearing statements like this of how you can't really be totally enlightened and be in the body. There's always some idea that enlightened teachers are only here maybe to help us, or maybe if one of them is here still, it's because they haven't really gotten it yet. So, I guess what I want to ask is, is that simply because they aren't integrated enough that they are saying these things?

A. H. Almaas: Are you saying those teachers say that it's not possible to be completely enlightened within a physical body?

S: Yeah. Or like, I forget which one it was, maybe it was Neem Karoli Baba, when he's about to die, saying, "Oh, now I'm released from central jail forever."

AH: But you could definitely experience the longing for it, for that complete release. And you could experience complete release a great deal, as the central thing in your life. Can you experience it completely, in all ways, all the time, every second? Well, that's a question. Is that possible when there's a physical body? Many people do say that it's not possible.

This question also implies that to be liberated means always being in the same state, like you are always divine love. But this is not what happens—in liberation, the state can change. It can be divine love or pure awareness or simply being or other ways we can be our true nature. The liberation means we are always true nature, not that we are always divine love. But that divine love is always accessible. We happen to be exploring true nature in its dimension of Divine Love.

S: That was an interesting exercise. My experience is I couldn't find anything that stopped me from wanting complete release. What I did discover was sort of a question of why don't I want it even more? It's almost like a question of how much passion do I have for the wanting? And in the exercise there was much more passion that was evoked. And it was interesting that even joking around, I said to my partner, "Come on. You've got it. And I want it. It's like you're holding it." It's as if it's someplace else. And it's obviously something I need to work on and look into more. But there's something about how much do I want it that seems to be the issue.

AH: Yeah. So, how much is part of it, definitely. So that's good. I mean that's what I'm sure happened for many people, because many people do experience that wanting, and when I say, "What stops you?" it might be that something's stopping you in terms of how intensely, how deeply, how fully you experience it. Many people have the passion for the truth, for liberation, but only few have it as a consuming passion.

S: I feel like I've been getting into more and more of a trap doing this work here. And I feel right now a lot of fear that's been building. Because it's like there is this trap: I want it, but I don't want it; I want it, but I don't want it. It's crazy making after a while. It's like I want it a lot, so then why am I stepping back from that? I want it with all my heart, and I don't want it with all my heart. And I feel like I'm in this dilemma, like an animal in a cage. I feel like this animal pacing around in a cage.

AH: Uh-huh. That makes sense, yes.

S: And one moment the dilemma is so funny. And the next moment it's the most painful, painful thing. And it's like, holding all of that, it's like kind of wanting to scream or something. You know, with the tension of it all.

AH: It is a dilemma. And whenever anybody gets to this place, they recognize the dilemma. The more the yearning intensifies, the more the fear of losing oneself rises and fights back. The yearning is to lose oneself in the truth, in the ocean of love and being. But even though it is liberation, for the ego self it is annihilation. And hence the conflict.

S: But I want out of it.

AH: So maybe that reflects your wanting that release, right? You say you don't want to have this dilemma. You want the release from it.

S: I yearn for it. And then I think the yearning and the wanting, the longing for that, is really more than wanting the actual experience.

AH: That might be. Right.

S: Because I might not be around to experience it.

AH: That's true. You might not be. So do you think that's a bad thing? That's the question.

S: Well yes, that is the question. How can I fully, fully invite it?

AH: You don't know. That's the concern; that if I really want that and I let it happen, I might not be around to know what it's like. Because you don't know what's it like when that kind of thing happens. Who's going to be around to experience it?

S: And as soon as I totally give up on wanting it and wanting to be around to experience that, then the wanter comes in more and holds on tight. And so I'm back in the dilemma.

AH: It's a dilemma where you find yourself in jail, right? In some kind of prison. But the prison walls are your own identity. So every time you assert yourself, you assert the prison walls. You see? Every time you say I want something, or I don't want something, you're asserting the prison walls. That's the dilemma. So all you can do is recognize that and understand it until you're completely convinced there is nothing you can do about it. That's the dilemma I was describing in my journal. You feel completely helpless. And you give up doing. You recognize it is not you who can do it. And then there is divine intervention. That's when divine love appears, as grace. But not before you are completely helpless. You see, that's the thing when people say, "Where is God?" God doesn't show up until you're completely helpless and accept your helplessness. As long as you don't accept that as a self you're helpless, as long as you believe you can do something or at least keep busy hiding your helplessness, the divine won't intervene.

S: But then ... Well ...

AH: That's the trap.

S: I'm sweating. I think I'm feeling more caged. And helpless.

AH: Very good. You just see the cage. I mean, for many of us maybe this work we're doing here now in this exercise will just show us the cage. And that in itself—if that happens—is quite enough. It's a lot, actually, just to see the cage and something of the nature of the cage.

S: But one thing I'm struggling with around this whole issue. If I give up the struggle and I feel the divine light, just when I finally feel like I'm letting go of that struggle and feeling the delicious presence, you know what happens then sometimes? It feels like my ego holds on even more tightly at that point.

AH: That will happen too. As long as you believe you can hold on to it, you will do that. Until you learn through repeated experiences that that's actually the way to lose it. When you try to hold on to it, you lose it.

S: It doesn't feel like "I" am trying to hold on to it.

AH: Yes, I know. It might not feel that way. So you just need to see, what is trying to hold on? See, if you remember what I read from my journal, I was feeling the helplessness, right? And then I realized, "Well there was nothing I could do, forget it." Divine love didn't appear right then. It happened a little while later when I was watching TV. The point of watching TV is that I forgot all about it, you see? I gave up, and I wasn't in the woods sitting there waiting. I really gave up, and said I might as well watch a Western.

S: For me this question brings up something about my relationship to the teachings. It's something I've been feeling while I've been listening to this teaching, and I feel a real sorrow about it. I can feel in myself all these little places of withholding and holding back. And as I was working on this question, I realized that withholding myself from really letting go, being fully with the questions that come up for me and being present—this withholding is directly related to my ambivalence about truly feeling the depth of my wanting and not knowing if it was ever going to be possible.

AH: That makes sense. So, the wanting and the longing is for the total and complete release, which, as I said, is really nothing but longing for that condition of divine love, which is the nature of everything. That love, that light, that freedom. So as it touches the soul from inside, the soul becomes activated, and it begins to awaken first as this longing, as this yearning. So one way of approaching and beginning to open to that divine love is to recognize this longing and to allow it to happen. And that means seeing all the barriers against it.

SIX

Jabba the Hutt

We're going to explore more deeply now the questions we've already looked at: What is the physical world? And what is reality in contrast to our usual experience of it? So to do that, let's take a closer look at our usual experience. What is the underlying position that the ego takes toward the world? And how does that then dictate the experience of the soul and its relationship to that world?

If we have experienced the boundlessness of being and recognized the whole world to be a manifestation of that beingness—experienced as presence, pure consciousness, love, or light—that will obviously challenge our view of physical reality. I've described the conventional viewpoint—that reality is purely physical—as being like that of an immature soul, meaning one who is like a child that believes the world is just the way the grown-ups have told her it is. But I'm going to focus on another metaphor now, one that distills more purely the position of the soul and its relationship to reality, when reality is seen from the viewpoint of the conventional world.

The conventional view is that there is just this physical world. It has your mommy and daddy in it, and lots of other different people. Some of them might love you and some of them might hate you, and some look similar to you and some don't. And as well as people, this physical world is full of various things that are either desirable because they bring pleasurable experiences or to be avoided because they bring unpleasant ones. This is the general scenario that society engages us in, and if you believe in these things, it will make you experience yourself and your relationship to the world in a certain way. It will make your soul appear a certain way, and that way is most clearly illustrated by the image of Jabba the Hutt. Do you remember Jabba the Hutt, who first appeared in the third Star Wars movie, *Return of the Jedi*? He is a giant slug-like alien who is a gangster and crime lord with an insatiable appetite.

I think Jabba the Hutt is a great metaphor or image to illustrate a manifestation of the soul that underlies the usual experience of the individual. It is a particular layer of the ego self that is a result of viewing the world as the source of all that we want and need. I'll tell you the experience that led me to this image, and then I'll elaborate on it.

This happened around the same time as the experience from my journal that I described in chapter 5, when I was experiencing the dimension of Divine Love and the boundlessness of light and love.

I wake up one morning experiencing a kind of negative merging, some kind of contraction that is painful at a very deep place in my body. As I explore it, I realize that the contraction is an expression of my belief in and focus on physical reality, and particularly the belief that the body is me. That creates a set of boundaries, and now as I begin to experience boundlessness, they appear in my consciousness as a painful contraction. I also realize that the attempt to be free from the contraction is the same as the contraction—the desire to be free from the boundaries is an expression of the belief in their existence, which only maintains the contraction. And as I'm dealing with all this, I become aware of the sense of an empty shell—the contraction now appears to be some kind of shell.

The empty shell is the experience of the personality when it's seen for what it is. When you begin to recognize that your personality is devoid of being, devoid of presence, devoid of essence, you feel like you're just a shell. There is nothing inside you—no substance, no fullness. And that usually arises when we are dealing with the question of identity: "Who am I?" "What am I?" This happens after you begin to work with and experience essence, being, or spirit. As we've seen, at some point, when you have had experiences of your essential nature, you realize that it's possible not only to *experience* essential nature but to *be* essential nature. Instead of experiencing strength, you are strength. Instead of experiencing truth, you are truth. So there's a shift of identity, and your sense of what you are changes. It's no longer as if I am this individual or self that is having an experience of spiritual presence. No, I *am* this spiritual presence. It's a fundamental shift in your experience of what you are, which is what we mean by "self-realization." The self-realization of essence or being comes when you experience it as your identity, as your center, as who and what you are.

So as we approach that self-realization, we start to experience our usual sense of self as a kind of shell with nothing inside. You begin to feel unreal, or fake, as you recognize that your usual sense of self is false. Having experienced your essential nature, you realize your familiar identity is not who and what you are but just an imitation. It's a mental construction made out of beliefs and images and their associated emotional patterns, which has resulted in you being something that is not what you are. Self-realization, by contrast, means just being yourself, which means being presence itself. So whenever the experience of the personality, the self, manifests as a shell that is empty inside, you know that you're dealing with the question of identity: "What am I?" And that arises at many levels. Every time you realize yourself as a new dimension of being, you will deal with another level of the shell of the personality.

So here the level of the shell related to divine love begins to arise for me. Through the contraction brought about by the experience of divine love, I have become aware of the shell but in a curious form that is different and new to me. The shell usually first appears as some kind of thick layer around yourself. Sometimes it's hard, like a walnut shell, and sometimes it's rubbery or wooden. It can manifest in different ways, and the way it appears usually reflects the dimension you're integrating. In chapter 5 I referred to a plastic boundary, which is such a shell. Here the substance of the shell feels curiously different. It feels a little fluffy, but I recognize that it's different from the fluffiness that's typical of love. It's like an imitation of the fluffiness of love, but I know it isn't that. And what it turns out to be is fluffy fat.

I can feel this big shell, about three or four feet thick, which feels like light, fluffy fat, so I'm feeling about four or five times my size. And that's when the image of Jabba the Hutt comes to me, because if you remember what he looks like, he's about ten feet tall and about five or six feet wide, and he's all blubber and fat. It's as if it's just a huge drop of fat sitting there, with no body structure. But what's interesting about the image of Jabba the Hutt isn't just its appearance and texture but what it reveals about a whole manifestation of the soul.

Now, I am not implying that the image of Jabba the Hutt is universal and that all human beings have it in precisely this form. Some women, for example, might find it easier to relate to a female version, which we could call Jabbette the Hutt, and other variations might arise in some people. But I find the figure of Jabba the Hutt to be a particularly powerful representation of this specific layer of our ego structure that exists in all of us. It is therefore a useful image to explore in detail here to get an understanding of this manifestation of the self.

So first of all, if there's all this fat, what does that mean? Well, fat means having extra, an excess. It represents an accumulation of more than you really need in the physical world, a physical accumulation that is in excess of what is required. And it's not only about feeling big and fat; I begin to have the experience of it also being about feeling greedy, feeling intense greed and lust. If you remember the character of Jabba the Hutt in the Star Wars movie, he had an intense lust for food, comfort, pleasure, power, control—all the usual worldly desires. And that's what I think the metaphor of Jabba the Hutt represents: complete worldliness. It's somebody who believes in the physical world absolutely and wants to get everything he can get from it. And what happens when you get as much as you possibly can in the physical world? You get big, you get fat, and you become a power mad rat. You try to control everything and be as powerful as possible, so you can get whatever you want.

You're lusty and gross and what you want is all kinds of crude pleasures, physical comforts, and possessions.

Contemplate this. Can you find a part of yourself that operates on these lines? Because this is what underlies our experience of ourselves. Underneath the veneer of being a civilized person, each one of us is Jabba (or Jabbette) the Hutt. If you believe the physical world is as most people, including most scientists, say it is, you are bound to be Jabba the Hutt. There's no other way, as it's a consequence of how the soul will relate to the world when it has lost touch with essence. How else could it be? If this is a world of disconnected objects, where some of them are sources of goodies and some of them are not, then you're going to become like Jabba. Because there's something here and not something there, right? The goodies are located in a particular place, and you're going to go and make sure you get them. You're going to try to get as much as you can of what makes you feel good, and you're going to feel the need for power and control in order to get it. And you're going to accumulate as much as you can of the goodies, whether they are possessions, money, people who love you, or different kinds of activities and pleasures that bring you gratification and satisfaction.

This is the place in the soul where there's a deep lust that is very physical and very gross. It's similar to a very primitive animal, but here it is a human soul, and when a human soul becomes animalistic, the animal instinct is exaggerated. Animals don't actually behave the way humans do when we say they're "behaving like animals"; for example, animals generally eat what they need, and then that's it, they leave it. They don't keep accumulating more and more, far more than they need. But when the human soul becomes like an animal, it just keeps accumulating more and more of what it wants. It tries to hoard as many supplies as possible, regardless of need. And this is what Jabba the Hutt epitomizes, being big, fat, greedy, and full of lust. So when we're caught by the illusion of the physical world and have the deep conviction that it can satisfy our needs, our soul becomes like Jabba—a fat, empty shell that lusts greedily for power, money, security, food, comfort, pleasure, and all the various goodies that people want from the physical world. Now, what do you call people who believe in physical reality and nothing else? Materialists. Empirical materialists. So in fact all empirical materialists are Jabba the Hutts in the depth of their identity.

It's interesting how the soul can manifest itself in this way, as mostly fat, representing excessive physical accumulation. I mean you can *literally* feel like a ball of fat. And as I said, the fat represents an accumulation of all kinds of physical things, so it's not just about the body getting bigger than it needs to be. The fat represents the hoarding of riches, possessions, and supplies and indulgence in all sources of gratification. It's only physical gratification, though. Not even emotional; simply physical. Jabba the Hutt is someone who is focused exclusively on the physical and believes only in the reified world. This dimension of the shell of the ego self is a result of relating to the world as purely physical, and it certainly doesn't involve a belief in anything spiritual. Jabba the Hutt doesn't believe in spiritual practice because spiritual experience offers him no physical gratification.

We've seen that this position of the soul stems from being an individual whose identity is based primarily on the physical body. You believe you're an entity with a separate body, with feelings and emotions, and sometimes even spiritual experiences. There is this physical world that you live in, and God, if there is one, lives someplace else. In the light of divine love, this individual entity is revealed to be the outer layer of most people's experience, and right underneath this layer is the experience of being Jabba the Hutt. This underlying entity is a more structured form of the animal soul—what I call the unregenerate soul. It believes there is something very positive about this physical world, because there are wonderful things to be found in different parts of it—goodies and riches to extract.

Now if you ever experience yourself as being like Jabba, it can make you feel grossed out, which is probably why you don't let yourself feel that way most of the time. But it is there, even if you don't feel it. And when you do experience it, you experience the source of all your physical excesses and overindulgence in things related to the physical realm—the need for physical objects as possessions for example, but also the craving for physical contact, physical warmth, physical comfort. It's all based on the belief that the physical world that is made up of objects and people is the only source of good things—there is no belief that God is the source of what you need.

However, if instead of being repulsed by this experience, you relate to it in the spirit of practice and view it as a curious and interesting phenomenon—if you are willing to look at it with a sincere and open mind—what you'll begin to see is that there's an underlying emptiness to it. And that's why, regardless of how much gratification you get, you never feel satisfied. This emptiness is what really underlies the experience of Jabba the Hutt, and it is why he keeps getting bigger. He may have accumulated all that fat, but of course it hasn't made the hunger go away. There's still an emptiness that's endlessly trying to feed itself from sources in the physical world and yet always remains unfulfilled. And this is the underlying experience of the worldly person. We may only get glimpses of it in ourselves and not recognize the full extent of it, but that is what's always there under the surface. Because this identification with physical reality and the physical body is so strong, it disconnects us from our true self, our true nature, and that leaves us with a feeling of emptiness. We try to get rid of that feeling by indulging in our excesses, but when we experience the manifestation of the shell, we can begin to allow ourselves to experience that emptiness for what it is.

So, back to my own experience.

I begin to feel the emptiness inside. The fatty external shell feels thick but also light and insubstantial. There are some tensions here and there in the body. The experience proceeds and by the afternoon it becomes mostly an emptiness, apart from the sense of a shield over the chest. As I let myself be Jabba the Hutt for a while, the emptiness dominates and the shell dissolves, leaving just the sense of a boundary. And then a curious perception occurs that reveals what the shell is about. The boundary feels continuous with external physical reality. It feels to me as if my personality and the physical universe make up one entity; my shell and physical reality operate at the same level and have the same significance. I recognize that being like Jabba the Hutt is part of experiencing the world from the conventional viewpoint. My shell is not separate from the physical world as I usually see it; it's a part of the world of objects, the world of separateness, the world of physicality, the world of particles—the reified world.

And then my experience of this reality, of me and the world, begins to lose its sense of significance. I begin to experience myself—especially my body—and the whole of physical reality, as empty and insubstantial. It's strange to see physical objects having no substance, no density. They're the same objects as before, but their physical reality seems different. They've lost reality and substance. They've become empty and flat. There's a flatness, a lack of color or vitality, which makes everything feel less real.

So this is what happens as we experience our essential nature; we recognize that who we usually are is just an empty shell, devoid of fullness, devoid of substance, devoid of significance. Just like a bubble. Before that, before your personality is challenged by essential presence, it feels real, right? It feels like there's you, and there's the reality of your body, your feelings, and your emotions, and you have substance. It's not essential, but it feels real and significant. Then, as essential presence expands and you start to recognize that your personality is all about images and identifications, you start to feel the insubstantiality of it—it becomes this empty shell, a bubble with nothing inside. This is what always happens when you recognize that something is just a mental construct.

And in experiencing the boundlessness of being, we have this recognition that it's not only the personality that loses its realness—the experience of the physical universe no longer feels real either. Before that, your ego gives both you and the physical universe some sense of reality. Your constructed sense of self is inseparable from your familiar experience of the world and so all of it appears to be real. This is the reality of Jabba the Hutt. However, when you go deep inside and contrast your usual experience of reality with essential presence, you see that there's nothing to it. And just as your sense of personality loses its color, brilliance and vitality as you recognize it to be an empty shell, so does your usual experience of physical reality when you experience a boundless dimension. It begins to lose its meaning, to lose its solidity, to lose its sense of vibrancy and aliveness, and begins to become flat, two-dimensional and empty.

So the central relationship of the individual to the world is that of greedy Jabba lusting after the physical world. More fundamentally, it is the empty shell of Jabba relating to what I call the cosmic shell. We see that the ego's world is as empty as the ego. It's a world devoid of God, devoid of being, and when you recognize this, the personal shell expands to become the cosmic shell. You see the whole physical world and universe as an empty shell, with nothing inside it. You begin to recognize that there's nothing there for you; what had been the source of everything isn't there any longer. And that is actually the way it is, but this truth is normally covered up in the experience of the individual by trying to fill the emptiness through extracting things from the physical world. It never works, you're never satisfied, so you keep wanting more and more and more.

This is true even in relation to the natural world. Every time you're in touch with yourself, your perception of nature changes. However, most people, even people who are nature lovers, still think a tree is a tree and a rock is a rock. After all, they're still separate objects. They just appreciate the beauty, the vitality, and the interconnectedness that exists in nature. However, it's coming from the same viewpoint as the most superficial level—just with some light coming through. The whole cosmic show of separate objects and the outside as the means to fill our inner emptiness is not challenged. When it is challenged, you recognize the whole universe, not just nature, to be an empty shell. We'll continue to explore why it's experienced that way. All I'm saying here is that just as you experience your personality as empty because it doesn't have essential nature, the world of this personality turns out to be empty as well, because it doesn't have essential nature either.

So I continue with the experience from my journal.

I become aware that I'm experiencing some kind of discontent because I'm not being myself. Earlier, I had been experiencing divine love and everything was love. And then everything was Jabba the Hutt. Now there is this cosmic shell and everything is empty. I know who I am, but I feel blocked from being my true nature. There's a lot of frustration. During the night, between fitful sleep and waking, I experience myself as the ego individuality. The shell comes back again and the state is like some kind of negative merging, a frustrated state. Then, as the boundaries begin to dissolve and become like dust, fine dust, I recognize that I am the problem here. I feel I am in the way. I feel I am the contraction and the cause of the contraction—that is, the belief in myself as a separate individual.

A couple of days later I become aware of what I call the pink stupa diamond, which is pink love appearing in diamond form. And that means it brings an understanding of love in terms of boundaries. It's the full understanding of what we've been exploring—the reality that love is not only my essence and my nature but the essence and nature of everything, including inanimate objects. Love is everything; everything is love. I begin to see sweetness and light everywhere. And I begin to understand that boundaries have no meaning and no existence in the dimension of love.

Now I see more clearly the connection between this true perspective and the state of Jabba the Hutt and the unreal universe. Just as the personality feels itself to be real, full, and existing, so it sees the physical universe as full, real, and existing. The sense of significance of the personality is continuous with the significance and absolute reality of the physical universe. When the soul takes itself to be a separate individual, it projects onto the world all its object relations from the past, and that projection is what makes it feel as if the world has some reality. It believes in the projection, just as it believes in the image of itself. Seeing the state of Jabba the Hutt means that there is now a perception of the truth about the personality—namely, that it is an empty shell of fat that it is full of greed, lust, and desire for physical pleasure, comfort, security, and power and is motivated by instinctual responses to a feeling of deficient emptiness, which is the lack of an essential nature.

Because this state of emptiness is continuous with that of the physical universe, both are now experienced as empty, flat, and lacking in significance or value. This realization comes when the fake filling of the emptiness is no longer present, which reveals the hole we have been covering up. The personality hole is part of what I call the cosmic hole, the hole in cosmic existence. This is the perception of the universe as deeply lacking once the projections of the personality onto it have stopped. When those projections are dissolved—just as your belief in who you are is dissolved—everything appears empty. The world and the whole cosmos appear empty. This is the cosmic hole, and because we're dealing with a boundless dimension here, this hole is boundless. We are seeing the personality hole as continuous with the hole in the universe. And when we experience and accept this cosmic hole, it can begin to fill with what we have been disconnected from.

The theory of holes that we use in this teaching describes the process of filling a lack in our soul through substitution, activity, or denial. When the filling with something other than what is actually missing is recognized and stopped, the lack or emptiness becomes apparent. This is what we call a hole in our consciousness: a place where some quality of our nature is not felt or experienced. Since the lack is painful or distressing, we cover it over by looking for a substitute or imitation on the outside to compensate for what's missing. Stopping the looking allows the absence to be felt again, and that emptiness, once fully acknowledged, becomes the space within which the lost quality of our essence can arise. As long as we are denying the deficiency or attempting to fill the hole, this can't happen.

So here, with this hole, the imitation is the usual experience of the personality in relationship to the usual universe. When we begin to question that, we start experiencing that we are Jabba the Hutt relating to the physical universe, which appears to promise instinctual gratification for our physical, animal nature. As we stay with our inner Jabba, we experience an emptiness pervading everything, as the cosmic emptiness, the cosmic hole, which is the hole of divine love. If we don't reject it but allow it to be, then the quality that we have lost begins to arise and fill this whole emptiness. The arising quality of love will show us that it is the true nature of everything, including the nature of the soul. Seeing that allows the experience of your true identity as this love that everything is made of. Everything appears as one thing, and you are part of it. The individual soul is inseparable from the ground of true nature, revealed as divine love. We will experience, then, the true fluffiness, not the fake fluffiness. Jabba's fat shell is fake fluffiness; it's the fluffiness of the physical level. But the true fluffiness is divine love, which is soft, sweet, real, and authentic, and it's light. It's light without being empty. When you're Jabba the Hutt with that fat shell, you may feel light, but that's because you're empty; there's nothing to you, really.

So we come back to the experience we've explored in earlier chapters, the experience of divine love being the nature of the whole universe, its molecular substrate. But now it comes through our perceiving the universe in a more accurate way. When we explore our personality and see it to be a shell, we can see our nature more accurately. Similarly, when we penetrate our usual notion of the universe and see the shell that it is, we begin to see the nature of the universe more accurately. We begin to see it as one undivided whole, without boundaries separating one thing from another. It is a nondual world. And the nature of the universe in this boundless dimension of Divine Love is one of delicacy, sweetness, and softness. We come back to the divine ocean again, but now it is not "I am experiencing it" but simply "it is experiencing." Now there is only one. There is no separate "I"; there is indivisibility. It's not that the physical world disappears. Things still appear to exist and interact, and the same patterns continue to arise, but they appear now as theophany, as manifestations of this divinity, which is boundless love and light.

When we experience the universe in this way, it doesn't make sense to take the position of Jabba the Hutt. There are no goodies to accumulate. It's all richness, everywhere. Abundance is everywhere and I am part of it, as an individual consciousness; I am one of the manifestations of this abundance. So what's the point of excess? Everything is infinite everywhere in the universe. If you recognize that the goodness and richness is infinite, that it's everywhere and not localized in any particular place, what's the point of needing power or control or possessing and accumulating anything?

That's why, when we experience divine love, it will put pressure on our personality and expose our Jabba the Hutt—the part of us that believes the physical world is disconnected and in separate compartments, some of which have goodies in them that we need to find and accumulate as much as possible. From the perspective of divine love, the whole thing is a goody. The whole thing is wonderful and sweet and loving. I don't need to get love from anywhere; everything is love. I don't need to fill myself with anything, I'm already full. The whole universe is full. But it's filled with appreciation, with consciousness, not with objects that you need to accumulate. And in truth, what's the point of accumulating objects if it's all one thing?

This brings a corrective to our whole worldview. We don't lose our sense of who we are—we're still human beings. But we are human beings that are expressions of this love. We begin to see ourselves and the universe in a more objective light, as what is truly there. There will still be chairs, trees, and cars, but they are nothing but manifestations of divine love. A car is a theophany. So is the ocean. So is your body. All of it expresses the divinity of existence. Divinity means that it's pure, it's harmonious, and it's sacred in the sense of not contaminated. It's not contaminated because it is as it is, in its original pure state, without being distorted by wrong ideas or beliefs.

So as you can see, the experience of the boundlessness of our being really begins to resolve our issues, our needs and fears, in a very fundamental way. You don't resolve the issue of love by working through the fact that your mother didn't love you, until finally you find somebody who does love you. That way of working out a solution is still within the delusion. It is good for therapy, but not for a spiritual path. The true solution is to recognize that you don't need anybody to love you. Everything is love, and you are love. If there's someone who loves you, and you love them back, that is part of the manifestation of that boundless love. You're just expressing it and living it. You're not "getting" it.

PRACTICE SESSION
JABBA THE HUTT
· · ·

This is a good time to explore your own experience of Jabba the Hutt. If you have a partner or partners to explore with, each of you will take fifteen minutes to do a monologue. If you want to, once your monologues are finished, you can discuss together what you discovered for fifteen minutes. If you are on your own, you can write out your inquiry for fifteen minutes.

Explore your sense of being an individual relating to the conventional, physical world. Look for the signs of an underlying greed and a lust for physical satisfaction: for pleasure, security, power, and any other kind of gratification. Those signs are everywhere, but they might be subtle, because we're very good at believing our delusions. Where are these self-centered desires and tendencies coming from? Look for the source of them and perhaps you will begin to see them as expressions of an underlying identification with Jabba the Hutt.

· · · · ·

Questions and Comments

Student: The whole time after I spoke in my triad, I tried to stay with the sensation of visualizing Jabba the Hutt and how it felt for me. And what I was really feeling in relationship to the image was that soft, fat, thick layer provided insulation for me. And then the image went on where, if you try and kill an animal that's got that much fat on it, you can pump a lot of rounds into it. It takes a lot to kill it. So you don't hit the vital organs without concerted effort, and so it provides protection. That seemed to be the strongest quality in that whole image for me. I realize now that I'm thirty pounds lighter than I used to be, there's not that sense of power and strength that I once had. Because with that excess weight I was also really hard, physically, and dense. I felt stronger inside that layer. And I also felt more independent and better protected than I do these days.

A. H. Almaas: Having the layer of fat as a protection is a particular issue that is not exactly the issue of Jabba the Hutt. The issue of Jabba the Hutt is like you're a fattened entity. If you remember the movie, it wasn't that difficult to kill Jabba the Hutt. In fact, the fact that he was so blubbery made it easy because he didn't move much. That brings in a good point here. When we're dealing with Jabba the Hutt and the big and fatty shell, we're not really talking about being physically overweight. That's not the point. You could be a very thin person, and when you experience Jabba the Hutt, you experience yourself as big and fat and all of that. So it does not really have anything to do with physical weight. You might have extra weight because of an identification with Jabba the Hutt, but not necessarily. There are other reasons why people gain weight. So you need to dissociate your physical weight issue from the issue of Jabba the Hutt. Jabba the Hutt represents excess in everything, everything that is physical.

S: The other thing that I got into was the fact that in areas where I do tend to be excessive, it's such a self-rewarding process, I can't see why I should give it up.

AH: It feels that way, like it's a self-rewarding process. Until you begin to know yourself and reality more and recognize it isn't really. The self-rewarding process of excess is an anesthetization. It is not a true fulfillment.

S: I became aware of two questions I wanted to ask you. One was some kind of splitting between the gross and the refined, between matter and essence. It seemed to bring up some question about that. And the other one was, when I was remembering the movie, the Jabba the Hutt that I remember was not just fat and hungry, there was a negativity and hostility. He wasn't just like a big fat baby at the tit, just wanting to suck, but there was this, like, nasty negativity involved.

AH: He was lusty in an aggressive way, in a selfish way. Very self-centered, very self-seeking, completely. That's true. That's good you bring that up. It's not necessarily that he hates people but that the hatred and anger is part of the lust and the greed and the power. It's one whole constellation. Because he is lusty, he doesn't care about killing people.

S: For me this experience of Jabba the Hutt was very, very oral, like a big huge mouth with a big huge esophagus and stomach that could never, ever be filled. And as I really let myself just kind of want to suck in everything—the world, clothes, jewelry, food, everything—the more I felt that, the more I felt the frustration of it, and that's where the rage came from. Just like feeding this continuous cycle of wanting more and then frustration because that doesn't do it and then wanting more. It's this bottomless hole, this bottomless pit, and all this sucking will never do it.

AH: That relates to the oral component of the shell, which is a particular deep structure in the ego self. Jabba the Hutt is more inclusive than that. There is an oral quality to Jabba, but not only an oral quality. When you get in touch with the oral quality of just wanting to fill yourself with whatever, although that is an element of Jabba the Hutt, it's a more primitive, early need. Jabba the Hutt has a little more of the sense of an adult being—it's more structured than the simple oral need. Also, the oral need doesn't differentiate between physical and nonphysical. It just wants everything, including emotional and spiritual experiences, while Jabba the Hutt is purely focused on physical things. Not only does he not care about other things, he doesn't even believe they exist. So it's a certain layer of the personality we're dealing with as Jabba the Hutt. I can understand that some of us will get in touch with other layers, which is fine. But I am working here with the particular layer of the ego self that emerges with the realization of boundless divine love.

S: I've had experiences of when I get really absorbed and am into presence, and there's like a part that looks at that and says, "But what is this good for?" And I'm wondering now if it is this part.
AH: Yeah. Might be. That's true. So that part, that's how it feels. Like, what is this good for?
S: It's a very peculiar experience to see all of that going on.
AH: That's good. So that's one of the expressions of Jabba the Hutt. Because it believes only in the physical world. And what

comes of the physical world. See, Jabba the Hutt is really a manifestation of the soul that many of the spiritual traditions try to deal with through renunciation, asceticism, celibacy, and all those kinds of disciplines in an attempt to not identify and go along with it. Obviously, however, if you really understand the situation we're talking about, those things don't necessarily work with Jabba the Hutt. All it means is that you're not acting it out. Doesn't mean you understand it. By renunciation and not having possessions, not having anything and trying to stay poor and not satisfy yourself, that will only work if it brings up into consciousness Jabba the Hutt and you recognize where those desires come from. And if you go through the understanding and the identification. But if you just do it as a moral and ethical discipline, it won't work. All it means is that you'll be a Jabba the Hutt who's hungry. But the renunciation or the celibacy can work if the not acting out is combined with understanding the source of the desires themselves, because then we'll become more aware of this internal identification.

S: Emotionally, in the inquiry and just now, sitting here, there's a certain kind of sadness that I feel. It's like I feel I'm touching on some kind of a hopelessness. And at the same time, I'm really seeing that there isn't any way out in that. That it's only by understanding it.

AH: Right. That's what we're doing; we're understanding the situation, so we expose the falsehood we believe is true. We don't try to change it; just uncover and understand it.

S: I feel a little concerned about what happened because I went into my lusts and my greed and my desires, and I got very into it. And then I experienced myself as a black panther, and then

I felt very powerful and lusty and greedy, and I'm going to get whatever I want. And I felt great about it. And it was very sleek and beautiful; not at all like Jabba the Hutt. So I felt, this is really cool, and I felt very identified with it, and I felt powerfully identified with it. I didn't feel like it was this disgusting blubbery thing. But then I realized that I've got my claws out and I'm totally identified with it. In other words, it didn't feel alien at all.

AH: So that sounds good. There are different layers of the lust and greed and all that. You went directly to the more animal root of it. Which will lead, then, to the black panther, the recognition of the sense of real power. Which, of course, you identify with; that's a good thing. Our soul can experience itself as a black panther, as happens in some shamanic teachings. It is not part of the ego identity but part of the potential of the soul. However, Jabba the Hutt is a different layer of the soul. It's the layer that is focused on that idea that it is the physical body, that the world is full of physical objects, and there are good things that can appear in one place or another. It's a differentiated layer that comes into being when the soul is structured by the conviction that the physicality of things is the truth of reality. It's different from the layer of just the animal—primitive, lustful, and wanting. Jabba doesn't feel animal and primitive when we experience it the way we're discussing it. It feels more like an adult human being. And there's a greasy quality to the whole thing. There's a feeling of a negative, greasy, full, and selfish human being, which is not as pure as the actual animal feeling.

S: That was what was confusing, because it felt, the animal feeling didn't feel like a negative feeling.

AH: No, it doesn't feel like a negative thing. While Jabba the Hutt is different.

S: Does this animal feeling have more of essence in it? Or is it just another delusion?

AH: No, this is not a delusion, unless you believe that that is all there is to you. But it's another story than the one we're describing here. From the various things people have said, we see that there are many levels of the shell that have desires and wants. And today we're dealing with a particular layer of it that has to do with the question of physicality.

S: My question is, so there's different layers of it? I'm not clear on tapping into or differentiating yet. I mean, I got into more the oral, and she's talking about the animal. This is more human, more adult, or whatever.

AH: The oral, or the animal, wants to consume things. Jabba the Hutt doesn't just want to consume things. He wants to have a big supply. The animal just wants to eat when it's hungry, and that's it. Jabba the Hutt doesn't just want to eat when he's hungry; he wants to have more than enough food there, lots of slave girls, lots of servants, lots of possessions, and lots of cannons around to dominate. Which is different from the oral thing, you see.

S: So there's some belief that that part can accumulate.

AH: Oh yes. With Jabba the Hutt, accumulation is a big part. That's what the fat means. It's accumulation.

S: When you talk about the accumulation, you also talk about power, where it's a less physical thing. And I was even, I was thinking about being seen, accumulating that. Accumulating those kind of less physical images.

AH: Jabba the Hutt is not interested in being seen. He's interested in being served. You do what he wants you to do. Whether you see him or not is irrelevant. You obey and do it exactly the way he wants you to do it. That's why the movie has dancing girls and gladiators fighting with the monsters to entertain him. That's what he's interested in. He's not interested in self-reflection. It might be useful to watch that part of the Star Wars movie. It can be helpful in understanding this part of the teaching.

S: So the power is a power to do things, not to have . . .

AH: Yes, it's a physical kind of power. A worldly kind of power. What I'm saying is, each one of us has that level in our soul. That's what we need to see. Because many of us, the areas we're going to are a little pure. We don't want to go as gross, as greasy, as Jabba the Hutt is. Well, I'm a primitive animal, a baby who just wants to eat. All that's true, but it's a little bit more pure than Jabba the Hutt. With Jabba the Hutt, purity is out the window. The concept doesn't even exist in his case. Jabba the Hutt, you see, doesn't feel needy.

S: I was feeling the lust and greed, and then I felt this fatty thing, like . . . have you ever seen pictures of people having liposuction done to them?

AH: Yeah, that's a good image.

S: I felt like that stuff that they suck out of your body. And this reaction that people are having is the reaction that I felt—revulsion. What I'm feeling now is what I felt then, which is, I can tolerate experiencing that identity and that presence, but I don't feel any of the lust. I feel so much revulsion that the idea of consuming anything feels really repulsive, and that's kind of like the maximum I can tolerate.

AH: You don't need to consume anything at the present time. You can just have more.

S: But I mean the feeling of greed or desire isn't there.

AH: So that might arise. Just stay with it. Just stay with that sensation. You're just feeling the quality of the fat. You actually might, if you get into Jabba the Hutt and feel the fat, you might become very specific as to what the fat is like. It's chicken fat.

S: I thought I'd mention this, since no one else has. And maybe no one else had this experience, but I was totally unable to get in touch with my inner Jabba the Hutt. Basically, the response that I seemed to have in essence was, I'm not Jabba the Hutt. And a strong determination, which I relate to an identification with scarcity, a denial of all those needs.

AH: I'm sure many people feel that way. That, of course, I'm not like that. They're much more refined than that. How can I be that way?

S: Right. I wasn't able to get any deeper than that.

AH: You could start from there. How that expresses Jabba the Hutt. That is one way to look into it.

S: I felt the most interesting part was that I saw that in order to understand my needs, Jabba the Hutt had to bring them out. And the more I bring them out, the more interesting they get. The more interesting they get, the more available the net result is. So I'm busy getting better and better at getting the need met, and so it gets less and less possible to see it as unreal. I thought that was an interesting dichotomy.

AH: Yes. The solution is to find the truth. What is the truth of your experience? When you're saying that you're getting your needs met, what does that mean? Does that mean there's no discontent? No dissatisfaction. If there is, where is it coming from? People in the world, many people feel they're getting some of their needs met. So it's not unusual for somebody to feel, well, yes, I'm getting this, I'm getting that. I'm successful. All that can happen. So you need to look very deeply into yourself. And to see whether that is complete. That's the lure of materialism. Materialism makes you feel you're going to get satisfaction. And you do feel it to some extent, as if you are getting something. And if you're not in touch with your essential presence, it will be difficult to see that the satisfaction you're getting is not actually real, not complete, it's not final. When the spiritual thirst is active, it usually reveals the emptiness of the kind of satisfaction you are talking about.

S: One of the things that I remember about Jabba the Hutt and about the lustiness of it is that he seems far removed from any sense of vulnerability or any sense of suffering. It's all yummy, yummy, yummy, yummy, yummy. Is there a flavor in there of pushing away suffering? Is it even close?

AH: Well, it's not a matter of pushing away suffering. It's more like from the perspective of Jabba the Hutt, if there's any suffering, he's going to do something about it. Somebody giving him a hard time, he's going to kill them. Right? If he wants something, if somebody's not going to give it to him, he's going to take it and kill that other person. That's what he does with suffering. He doesn't deal with it inside. So that's true, there's no sense of vulnerability. There's this sense of bigness and power. That I can do it, and I'm in charge.

S: In some way, to me, I just keep thinking it feels like the beast because it's so . . . you know, it's the beast having a good time. There's something beast-like about it, in the sense of total annihilation of everyone else but my own self-interest.

AH: An identification with physical satisfaction. Seeing physical satisfaction as all the possible satisfaction for a human being.

So that way a person, the moment they're aware of a little dissatisfaction, they just do something else. Get more. That way you don't get to feel that the dissatisfaction might have other sources. And that way of greed, or that way of trying to satisfy oneself, part of what it does is anesthetize you from seeing that the physical world is not all there is. It keeps supporting the reification of the world. If you begin to feel the dissatisfaction that comes from the fact that the physical world doesn't give it all to you, if you see that dissatisfaction, that will begin to challenge that worldview.

SEVEN

The Real World

You can experience reality, existence, in many ways. And we're seeing that one of the main ways of experiencing it is as pure love, pure unadulterated presence, which is love that is light at the same time. Divine love is consciousness, light, and love, as one infinite medium. We can experience all of reality as this love and see that it is the very nature of reality. When we see that, we recognize that notions such as "absolute evil" don't make sense. There's no such thing, because the nature of *everything* is that love. So even if there is evil, its nature, ultimately, is bound to be love. Yes, it may come out in some kind of distorted way at times, but the building blocks of reality are always love. Just like the building blocks of the body are protoplasm—whether the organs that you have are healthy or sick, they're all made of the same protoplasm.

This perspective shows that the various people who've tried to explain the world in a dualistic way haven't seen reality as it is. Or at least, they have not seen this particular important way in which reality can be experienced. For instance, we know that many teachings and philosophies think of the world and the divine as two separate things. There are a lot of people who ask, "How come God created a world that is the way we know it? Why would any god feel the need to create a physical world, full of things like rocks and animals, with all the fighting and killing and the suffering and pain that comes with it?" So that's why, for instance, the Gnostics believe that the physical world is the creation of a lesser god, the demiurge, that came into being through a corruption of the divine spirit. The real God, as they see it, is one of absolute transcendence, beyond anything incarnate, so it was this lesser god who created our troublesome world in a spirit of vengeful rebellion. It's a way to explain the world, you see, just as with some of the Hindu philosophies that say the world is an illusion.

But when we understand the boundless dimensions, the boundless world of being, we recognize that the world we live in is actually an expression of the purity of being. We begin to see that the physical world—and even the world of strife, pain, and suffering—is not a separate world from divine being, because it's not separate from love or awareness. The physical world *is* the divine being but seen from a limited perspective. It's the same with the human being, the human soul. You can experience yourself from a limited perspective or from an open perspective. If you look at yourself from an open perspective, you are light, a body of light. You are presence, you are fullness, you are consciousness, you are beingness. If you look at yourself from a limited perspective, the perspective of your images and identifications, you become the clunky physical body that has a problematic personality.

So just as there's a real self and a false self, there is a real world and a false world. Just as the usual personality is the false self, the usual world is the false world. And the real world is not somewhere else, just as the real self is not somewhere else. It's just a matter of a correction of one's perspective. Looking at things without obscuration, we begin to see the world as it is.

And I think it's wonderful that when we begin to see the world as it is, we can see it in one of its main potential manifestations: as pure love. Pure delight, pure gentleness, pure softness. And it's good to spend some time approaching and experiencing the world from that perspective. We can also see the world as awareness and emptiness, which are more sober, less heart-centered ways of experiencing it. But here we experience reality as love, delight, softness, and freedom. We can see and appreciate the world as a place of rejoicing, of singing and dancing, playing and having fun, because that is also one of the inherent ways of experiencing reality. That's why in the Indian tradition they have Brahman, the formless, changeless, and mysterious ultimate deity underlying reality, but they also have Krishna, a childlike deity who goes around playing pranks and seducing humans with music and ecstatic dancing. Krishna is one manifestation of Brahman, expressing its playful and loving quality. Similarly, in Kashmiri Shaivism, there is Shiva and Shakti, and the world is the creation of Shiva, expressed through Shakti.

So when people say the world is an illusion, we want to understand what that means. Is the world really an illusion? Or is it that we hold on to an illusion that makes us see the world in a false way? The people who hold that the world is an illusion believe that nothing exists apart from the ultimate truth, and the world you see is just your beliefs, your ideas—constructs in the mind. A lot of modern thinkers think that way, that if you dissolve the constructs in your mind, there'll be nothing left. But what we see is that if you dissolve the constructs in your mind, what remains is the true structure of the world. We recognize that those constructs of the mind have just been overlaid on the appearance of the universe. As a result of that overlay, we start to see the universe in a way that is no longer direct and objective. It's the same with our soul; when we overlay a self-image on it, we start seeing it in a way that is not true—it's distorted.

As we explore our personal experience, looking at how our soul became an ego, our personality, we learn that this happens gradually, starting from our early experience. It starts with the impressions we receive in our early relations with parents and others, from which we form various images and impressions of ourselves. These gradually build up into object relations and then into an overall structure. At some point we have a general image of who and what we are, which remains mostly unconscious but structures the soul in such a way that it appears as what we call our personality. So we become this separate individual with a past, because that separate individual is formed by the images from that past.

But as we've seen, it is also known from developmental psychology that in the development of the ego, we don't only develop an image of ourselves through our object relations; we also develop an image of the other—initially the primary caretaker, the mother for instance, and also the father. We develop these images of the other—the object in object relations—and as we grow up, they include an image of the whole world. We develop a representation of ourselves from our early experiences and along with it, a world representation is developed as well.

So from all our early experiences—of our holding environment and the adequacy or inadequacy of it, and the interactions with the people around us—we develop certain memories that coalesce. This creates a structure in the ego that is usually referred to as the "representational world". What this term reflects is that in our mind we have an image of ourselves, but we also have an image of the world, of reality "out there." Each one of us has such an image, each slightly different, but there are some basic elements common to everyone's image of the world, just as the basic image of being a separate individual is common to all of us.

The soul therefore develops an image of itself and an image of the world. When it looks at itself through its own image, it becomes a personality. When it looks at the world through its image of the world, the world becomes the conventional one. In other words, the world that most people experience is a representational world; it is reified, meaning a world that has been fixed within certain concepts, within certain images, or rather within a certain constellation of images. This conventional world is a constellation of images, impressions, ideas, concepts, and beliefs that make up our whole worldview.

So you don't just develop images of yourself and your mother but of the whole environment that you and your mother are in. We each develop a different sense of the world as we grow up and become adults, according to our own experience. Some of us felt, and continue to feel, that the world is more trustworthy than others feel it is, for instance. Some of us see the world as empty or as impersonal. Some of us see the world as harsh and violent. Some of us think of the world as positive and generous. Everyone's view is different. But there is nevertheless an implicit feature underlying the general world image, just as there is an implicit feature underlying the different content of our self-images. Part of your self-image might be to think, "I'm a bad girl" or "I'm an angry boy"—whatever the image is that you've developed of yourself. Everybody's got their own images, but at the base of it all, everyone develops the sense that they are a separate individual with an identity. And it's the same thing with the representational world. We all develop different images of the world, but there is one thing common to them all: the view that the world is atomized. We all believe that the world is composed of separate physical objects. This is true regardless of whether one considers any given element or pattern that one is seeing as true or false.

When we begin to experience Jabba the Hutt, we're basically getting a little deeper into our experience of our self-image and the world that this self-image relates to. We begin to experience our sense of self as empty because it's just an image—it doesn't have any substance. Then we also recognize that the world is empty. But again, it's the image that's empty, not the real world. It's our representation of the world that turns out to be empty, just as our representation of ourselves is what's empty.

An image is an empty thing; it's nothing but a mental picture. So that's why, when we experience our soul through the image of our ego structure, at some point we always find an emptiness in it. There is nothing there, because that's the nature of a constructed image. And it's the same with the world. For a long time we don't realize that the world we're experiencing is simply a result of the filter we're looking through. We think that's how it really is. And most scientists take it to be that way too. In general, scientists do not look beyond the belief that the world is composed of objects, although there are theories now that challenge that.

When we experience ourselves as empty, as a shell, we're recognizing that we've been seeing ourselves through an image, a representation created through time by the mind. And when we see that the world is empty, it means we are penetrating our image of the world. But we're still not really seeing the world, because the real world is not empty; it is not an illusion. It's the representational world that's the illusion. Throughout history, when mystics and spiritual seekers have come to feel that the world is an illusion, that it's not real, that it's all empty, it's understandable that they have taken this emptiness to be the nature of the world. But it's not the nature of the world; it's the nature of the images that we have in our mind.

The illusion of the world is a much more difficult one to penetrate than the illusion of ourselves, because it's an illusion that our whole society supports with great conviction. Society says, "Yes, of course, this physical world is real and it's easy to prove it. The world is not just composed of our images of it. If you don't believe it, I'll just throw a rock at you. And that really hurts, doesn't it? See, reality *is* physical!" And we're satisfied with that kind of "proof." But what about the reality in your dreams? When you're dreaming and somebody hits you with a rock, it hurts, doesn't it? People can wake up from a dream like that because the pain is so strong. But was there a rock that hit you? Of course not. So you see, it's easy to poke holes in the physical, materialist theory. Not that we're trying to poke holes in anything. We're not trying to make a case. We're just trying to understand reality.

In the previous chapter, we discussed and explored the nature of the physical world experientially from the perspective of Jabba the Hutt, from which we believe that the physical world is the source of our satisfaction. And how, if we look into that more, we begin to see the emptiness of that world and its illusory promises. Now we're understanding it in a more psychological way. We've learned that when we see the world as well as ourselves as an empty shell, it means we're beginning to see the representation we have of the world. That's why I mentioned in the account of my own experience, when I started experiencing my shell and its emptiness, that I saw it was an extension of the world. It felt like my shell wasn't separate from the physical world. Now, it's clear that the shell is a mental construct, so right away that told me that the whole world, the way I'd been seeing it, is also a mental construct.

But we're also seeing that this does not mean the whole world is nothing but a mental construct and that there is no real world. It just means that the world as we know it is a mental construct. And as that is dissolved, we begin to see the true structure of the world, its true pattern, which exists and can be perceived. When you deconstruct your representation of the world, the real world can manifest. And that cannot be deconstructed, because the representational self is no longer there to do the deconstructing.

If we put together all that we've been exploring, we can see how our representational world, what we believe the world to be, developed from our interaction with our early environment, the people in it, and what they believed. And what that world became is based primarily on the notion of separateness, rooted in the experience of our physical body being separate from other bodies. That gave you the idea of being separate from all the other separate physical objects around you. And soon you learned that some of the objects are called humans, and some of them are important sources of life, because they're the sources of some kind of goodies that you need. Then you learned about other physical objects that are sources of some kind of satisfaction, and others that are sources of pain and difficulties. And of course, there's a lot in our experience of reality that contributes to this idea of how the whole world is constructed. Yes, things do look different. Things do feel different in different places. So it's natural that we develop the "easy" point of view that the world is dismembered, full of separate objects, good and bad. And since you are in this physical world and have to survive in it, then of course you'll go about getting the good things from the good places and trying to avoid the bad things from the bad places. But when we live by that perspective, we are just perpetuating and making more real to ourselves our representation of the world. Which means we continue to support a false way, or more accurately, a limited way, of viewing and experiencing the world.

So it's not surprising that this conventional way of experiencing the world is powerful and difficult to penetrate. It's so entrenched and crystallized because all of society supports it, and it's all you've known for as long as you've known anything. It's a powerful, cemented conditioning that is very difficult to shake off. Even when we see reality as it is—a different reality in which everything is light and illumination, brilliance and love—it's hard to keep to that way of seeing. Because something passes, the atmosphere changes inside you, and then you're back in the familiar "reality" of the physical world of separate objects. Having returned, you believe that you've just had an interesting experience instead of recognizing that, no, that wasn't an experience, that was a peek at true reality. We're so convinced of the physical, materialist view of reality that we easily fall back into experiencing it, reaffirming our conviction that it is true.

The problem is that this materialistically reductionist view becomes the basis for our soul to believe in the validity of its greed, its desires, its lust and aggression, its attachments and prejudices, and its negativity. Because the moment the world is dismembered, then one part can be against another part. And the problem is not only the dismemberment but that the love that unifies is no longer there. From the purely materialist viewpoint, there is no implicit love that makes you feel good toward other people and that can overcome the separateness. And where there are two without love, there can be conflict. So it's the belief in that dismembered world that creates Jabba the Hutt in us and keeps us identified with that position. It supports the belief that our insecurity, our need for accumulation, and our need for power and control are all real. It reinforces the idea that you should try to satisfy these needs, because that's the only way to support and protect yourself and achieve a state of satisfaction. So of course, most of the world believes that this is what will bring them security, happiness, contentment, and a sense of fulfillment in life.

But people have a Jabba the Hutt and then a little bit of superego—the rigid morality of the ego self—on top, and that's what keeps Jabba the Hutt under wraps. That's why most people try to behave in ways that are a little bit more civilized. In some sense, when you look at the present situation in the world and see all the difficulties we face—crime, terrorism, racism and prejudice, and ruthless exploitation of not just other human beings but the planet itself—you might wonder if it's all getting worse. If that's true, I wonder if it's because humanity is a little freer from the superego. There's certainly more licentiousness in the world than there was a couple of generations ago. People don't feel such a need to be civilized, to be "good" anymore. And if people don't feel that way, then they are freer to express themselves. And what will come out first? Their Jabba the Hutt.

So maybe the superego protected us for a long time and that protection isn't there as much now. Which means that if we really want to deal with our problems and those of the world in a way that works, we need to find something more real than the superego. We need to understand the structure of Jabba the Hutt and its related structures to see what they're really all about. We need to be able to penetrate until we see reality as it is, so that our more civilized and compassionate behavior arises as a direct expression of the truth.

PRACTICE SESSION
YOUR WORLD AND YOUR NEEDS
. . .

Now you have an opportunity to further explore the representational world, the image of the world you have developed along with the image of yourself. Each person will take fifteen minutes to do a monologue, working with one or two other people if possible. If you are on your own, you can take fifteen minutes to write out your inquiry.

Inquire into your belief in the world of separate objects, which has goodies in some places and bad things in others. Consider the following questions:

What do you feel you need most in the world? What do you hope and desire to get from it? What do you feel the world will give you?

Do you think these things will bring contentment and fulfillment? If so, what makes you believe this?

What is there in this world that you feel a great need to avoid? Why?

What does all this reveal about your deepest beliefs and feelings about the world?

Can you get a sense that the world your Jabba the Hutt believes in is not the real world but a false and empty

image—a world of separate entities, which is devoid of
the love and light that is everywhere?

Do you ever see, or at least get a glimpse of, the real world
behind this false one? What about now?

· · · · ·

Questions and Comments

Student: What struck me is that there seems to be another wisdom about reality that is covered over. This has to do for me with mortality. It's like Jabba the Hutt, the one thing he lives in big denial with is that he's going to die one day.

A. H. Almaas: Right.

S: And it seems like, through the ages, our mortality has worked to jar people out of this identification with the physical world. And so when we said earlier that there's an intelligent feature to reality, that it has the manifestation of divine love because it eases a soul's transition from identification as an individual to something else, in a similar way this mortality struck me as like another wisdom like that, that helps us detach.

AH: That's true.

S: In the second question I had the experience first of being so exceedingly fortunate that the world gave me everything that I needed. And then what happened is that the other side started creeping in, which is actually my mother's view of the world, of utter despair, desolation, destruction, pain, suffering. I had a realization that both of those were very precarious realities. And then I realized that I actually had an awareness in this moment that saw that split, which seemed to be more substantial. But it wasn't the experience of the reconciliation of that split. And so my question is about what you said earlier, that when one sees the world as it really is, there is just divine love. And that the experience of the evil isn't substantially real in the same way. I'm curious about that. I need something that gives me a sense of how that can be resolved. I've read many mystics, and they all speak about it being resolved ultimately, and they have that awareness. But I'm curious about your own experience, if you could say something about how, through your awareness, you came to the realization that there was only divine love and how you experienced that through the sort of negative experience with the evil or whatever.

AH: It's like, what is the focus? What is the focal setting for your perception? You see, if the focus is on the innermost nature of reality, you realize that this reality is goodness itself. And that's everywhere, and it is everything. When the focal setting is more on the surface, on the manifestation, it appears then as the physical world with all its difficulties. So it resolves it for me. It does not necessarily resolve it for somebody else. For it to resolve for somebody else, they have to see something similar to what I'm seeing. That doesn't mean, when I say it's resolved for me, that I don't see negativity, I don't see aggression in the world. There is suffering. Obviously, the world is full of pain and suffering and negativity. Right?

S: Could you give a specific example of how you had that awareness?

AH: Remember what I read from my journal earlier? That was an example of feeling the emptiness of everything. And within that emptiness, when I accept it, it begins to fill in with the softness, with the sweetness. And before I know it, I realize this sweetness doesn't just pervade everything; it constitutes everything. It constitutes the murderer as much as the saint.

S: There seems to be a difference between emptiness and evil, destruction, suffering, and killing, so how, if one goes through that experience, can it lead to an experience of divine love? **AH:** Well, we do that all the time by working on our issues. When you work on your issues, you're working on your identifications with part of yourself from the past. You work on being angry or hateful or afraid and such things. And as you understand them, those parts reveal a deeper part of yourself. And before you know it, as you understand these things, then the love or whatever quality arises. So if the person who murders really, really works on themselves, they will be able to experience their nature as love. But if they don't work on themselves, they will continue to believe their wrong viewpoint. They'll be taking a delusion as real. And we know the delusion determines your experience—what you believe is what you experience. So a person who believes that the world is out to get them, that's what they see. And they're gonna feel justified in protecting themselves by killing people. But if the same person understands that and sees what that's about, where it's coming from, and recognizes their identification, they will also be able to see that underlying all of that is the need to be loved. And when they deal with that need to be loved, they'll recognize that there is love there.

S: Well, I'm thinking of my mother, who was in a concentration camp and was very much a victim, and I just would imagine that it would be very difficult for her to see that, by just looking at her object relations, that it would necessarily give her the experience of the world as divine love.

AH: It's possible. There are people who have done it. There are stories about people who were able to actually use the experience of being in a concentration camp to begin to experience love in some universal way. It's not easy, definitely. Most people don't do it. But it's possible. The fact that it's possible attests to its truth. The fact that it is not common does not mean it's not true; it means it's difficult. And for somebody who understands it, who experiences it, that person will recognize that it's difficult for most people—for almost everybody—but that it is true, that it is possible. It is definitely a perspective that is very hard to accept, because our usual experience is so overwhelming, seems so real, so solid, right? So if somebody shoots you, even if you're experiencing yourself as divine love, you'll begin to bleed. However, if you're experiencing divine love, you'll recognize that the blood is made out of love. Experiencing everything as divine love doesn't mean you won't bleed. It means you'll bleed, but the blood itself will be divine love. So will the bullet.

As I've said, love or boundless being is the nature of things. When I say the nature of things, that means the inner constituency of things—just like the inner constituency of the physical body is protoplasm. And the cells can be healthy or not healthy, but they're still made out of the same thing. How they manifest depends on the pattern that determines their development, but they're always made out of the same thing. So if that was the focal setting for you, you could continue seeing the protoplasm all the time that you're seeing a particular part of the body and that would be the same as seeing divine love in everything, regardless of what happens. When you do that, you'll tend to be more loving, you'll tend to be less aggressive, more helpful and compassionate. And the more people do that, the more that love will be expressed. It's definitely a subtle thing and doesn't make logical sense according to our usual experience. So that's why, when the realized person bleeds, they bleed love.

S: I had a really interesting experience with that second question. The world couldn't give me what I need—exterior worlds seem to have no reality at all. At the same time, there was not a belief that I could give myself what I need, but not a total disbelief that I couldn't give myself what I need. It's sort of like an in-between, and yet I have never had the experience that I can really give myself what I need. As that continued to develop, I kind of got to the place that had a question: "Do I need to be physically alive to be?" That was where it seemed to all come to. That seems to have a kind of . . . I wouldn't call it exactly fear, but certainly it's a . . . slight tremulousness or a shakiness about that whole thing. And it's almost like, "Do I have to have this physical body to continue to be?" That seems to be a question. And the other question is, "What if I get to some place further and further along, where the only place to be complete would be to physically die?"

AH: Some people end up believing that, that to be complete is to physically die. But you say you have a body. The way I see it is you don't have a body. You know why you don't have a body? There isn't a body to have. And not only that . . . there isn't a "you" that can have a body. It is all one ocean of presence that has patterns, or shapes, in it. And all of it has consciousness. Part of the shape says, "I'm here, this little shape is me, separate from the rest." The more you separate yourself that way, the more the whole thing begins to dismember and appear as spots and islands and physical things. And then the logical thing that arises from that is that you have a body. It's a complete reversal of the point of view that really sees what boundless being does to reality. Our thinking in terms of empirical materialism is so deep. Even people who call themselves idealists, who believe in ideal philosophy and in being spiritual, they still basically think as if they are empirical materialists. That the material world is real in an ultimate way. Because they continue behaving that way.

S: That's really helpful, because it's clear that I can have the experience, the so-called physical experience, of feeling boundless and at the same time think, "I'm alive." It's like, this body will die . . . It's helpful, thank you.

AH: Yes, the body will die, that's true. But think of it this way: In your inner experience, don't certain manifestations of presence come and go?

S: Absolutely.

AH: The body is one of them.

S: That's easy for you to say.

AH: If you think of it that way, then when the quality of presence that we call the body is there, we say, "I'm alive," and that means this and that, you see? Which is fine, that's what fits that manifestation of presence.

S: That's true. Thank you.

S: These questions kind of drove me crazy. I had a really hard time answering them, especially, "What's the world going to give you?" And also about need. And it's just, all I could get to was something about this perspective of the world and me. That seemed to be what the whole question was about.

AH: Yes, it is, yes.

S: It was all about perspective, literally. That when I thought there was a world and me, then there could be these questions. But when I didn't think the world was separate from me, there was no question to answer.

AH: Those questions are meaningless then. So it's the questions that self-destruct.

S: And all I wanted to do was leave while it was self-destructing on me. It was hard to sit with it, I kept getting sleepy, I kept hating the question, I kept wanting to get up, but it all kept coming down to, well, if I am the world, I have everything.

AH: Right. Exactly. You have everything, you are everything.

S: I had the same thing happen. But I thought further. I don't personally have too many experiences of being the world. But it seems like the whole concept of time would be, you know, you always hear that in reality there is no time, there is no space. And it seems that if you are the world, or in that experience, that there would be nothing that would happen that you didn't know was going to happen. No more mysteries, no more . . . you would know the future.

AH: That's possible. The more, the fuller, your experience that you are reality is, the more you'll see. But there are different subtleties and depths of that realization. So just experiencing "I am the world" doesn't necessarily give me what's going to happen in the future. That's another, deeper realization. To experience that I am the world is one thing. To continue experiencing it that way is a whole other thing. Just like when you're experiencing essence at the beginning, you have an experience, but to keep it, to walk around with it and function with it is not easy. It's a much bigger step. The same thing with experiencing the boundlessness. At the beginning you can have the experience, but then, how to realize it, how to continue it, how to live in that perspective? That's not easy. In fact, most people throughout history took the position that you just have a few experiences of that, and that's it. Many of the famous thinkers, that's all they had. Plotinus himself said he had the experience of unity two or three times in his life. And he built a whole system that affected three religions.

S: So it's like it becoming a station.

AH: Yes. To become a station is not an easy thing. And the more you become a station, the more you begin to see and understand and have various capacities.

S: One thing I came across in these questions was how much I took for granted in my notion that I understood what the world was. And as I tried looking at that, I started realizing that I believed a lot about the world, but that didn't make it fact, whatever fact might be. So, I came to the conclusion that it was in my upbringing, the way in which I used my perceptual apparatus and my mind was trained and dictated to me, because I always harbored a belief that something wasn't being told to me. Things were not all that they were telling me they were. There was something bigger, different, there had to be more. That's the only thing I can figure that led me to even being in this school. And so beliefs, I feel, are shaped around somebody shaping the way I use my perceptual abilities. So, to see beyond that is a lot like being raised in a room painted white my entire life and then, when presented with concepts of the boundless, being told that there's something outside of that room and it's a big surprise to me. I only know how to live in that one room, and that becomes the whole construct of reality and how I function in it.

AH: That's a good way of putting it. I've called it "empirical materialism." I think another term that is used for it is "naive realism." That's the conventional view of physical reality. You take it the way you learned to perceive it when you were young.

EIGHT

The Personal God

When working with the boundless dimensions, I use a language that I tend not to use otherwise. It's more of a religious language, using terms such as "God," "divine being," or "divinity." I don't usually use those terms because it's very likely that people will misunderstand what I mean by them. That's because they are widely used and everybody has their own associations to them, which determine what they mean when they use them and what reactions are triggered and what feelings are evoked when they hear them. But when I use these terms, I use them in a very specific, very precise, and very exact way. I use them to mean specific things that are part of our work in the Diamond Approach. And it's only when it comes to the boundless dimensions, at least in our work, that it becomes possible to use this terminology and understand for the first time what these words actually mean.

The terms I usually use to refer to the spiritual realm are "soul," "essence," "being," and "true nature." And when I try to differentiate between the nature of the soul and the nature of the world, I usually talk about essence and being in the sense that essence is the nature of the soul, while being is the nature of existence. In the end they're the same thing, as we see in Hinduism, where Atman is the nature of the self and Brahman is the nature of existence, with a major focus of Hindu spirituality being the identity between Atman and Brahman. Using the words "essence" and "being" gives us a more neutral terminology. They are terms that most people don't use, and so they help to avoid some of the difficulties that arise with words that have emotional associations from our childhood and our religious and cultural background.

One meaning of "being" is the way philosophers use it, meaning "being as such" rather than a particular being, so referring to the mode of existence of all beings and all of reality. That's one way I use it, but I also use it to mean the nature of everything, because in the Diamond Approach we understand that the nature of everything is its beingness. So if I use additional terminology such as "God," "divinity," "divine being," or "supreme being" when discussing the boundless dimensions, they are just qualifications of the word "being" that I've already been using. And when I say "divine being," I don't necessarily mean what most people think of when they hear those words, which is God. That might be what I mean sometimes, but bear in mind there are probably around four thousand religious denominations in the world today, each with its own view of what God is. So everybody's got a notion of God from their own upbringing and what they've learned from church or synagogue or wherever. People have all kinds of ideas about what God is and what God isn't, and they don't necessarily correspond to what I'm referring to.

When I say "divine being," I mean being that is the nature of all reality appearing with the quality of divine love, the dimension of loving light that glows and has a sense of heart to it, a sense of purity. Since I refer to this dimension as Divine Love, and being is the infinite ground appearing as any of the boundless dimensions, I put the two together to refer to divine being. I'm not saying that being *only* appears with that quality, but when it does have this quality of love and tenderness, lightness and joy, then I call it divine being, and so by that I basically mean "being as such" that is manifesting with the harmony of love implicit and inherent in it.

You'll notice when we go to other boundless dimensions that I won't necessarily use the term "divine being." I might use "supreme being," for instance, if I'm talking about the dimension of pure presence—what I call the Supreme dimension. And it's true that what I call divine being or supreme being is taken to mean God in many teachings—mystical traditions in particular tend to take the experience of being to be the experience of God.

I grew up in a traditional religious Muslim family, but I wasn't religious at all. I'm still not. Even though most of my family were religious and prayed devoutly, there were exceptions, and I was one of them. In a Muslim country, all the way through school you have to do religious studies, read the Koran and study stories about the prophets. But from the beginning I mostly didn't buy what I was learning. I didn't believe it because it didn't make sense to me—my attitude was more scientific and experimental. It wasn't necessarily that I believed there was no such thing as God, but the God that most of the teachers were talking about seemed to be just a reflection of a human being's mind. It was too anthropomorphic and too pedantic for my taste. I thought that if there was a sacred reality, it should be something better than that.

That was my insight, and it meant that I basically didn't pay much attention to religion. I passed my religious studies classes, but I was not a religious person, and I wasn't a spiritual person either. I didn't disbelieve religion or spirituality, nor did I believe it; it just wasn't of any concern to me. I had no interest in it because I had no experience of it—I didn't have any recognizable or explicit spiritual experiences until I was in my twenties.

When I was a child, my early spiritual experiences were too subtle for me to recognize as something notable, though I did recognize their significance later in life, when I encountered such experiences again. Many people talk about all the spiritual experiences they had as a child, but I had none of the kind that people usually report. I was just a regular person having a regular experience of the world. Yes, I'd heard about God, but I didn't know what to think about it all. And that was about it.

So my conscious interest in spiritual studies didn't start until much later in life, when I was twenty-five or so, and I didn't have what I knew to be a spiritual experience until I was twenty-six or twenty-seven. But when I look back at my life, I realize there was in fact a religious thread in the experiences that were arising in me as I was learning about myself and reality. This was different from my spiritual experience as it developed, which was generally more of a mystical kind. And that's what we have in the Diamond Approach, a more mystical orientation: to experience and look into the nature of yourself and the nature of reality. To look for the truth that is beyond one's personal conception of truth.

This meant that for a few years at the beginning, even when my spiritual opening was underway and I was having all kinds of experiences and insights and realizations, I still didn't think about God or divinity one way or the other. But once in a while I would notice that other thread running through certain experiences I was having. I was experiencing essence and various aspects and learning about essence and true nature, but there were also occasional experiences of feeling what people call a sense of nearness. I felt that I was nearing some kind of ultimate truth, and although I didn't know what it was, it involved the heart more than anything else.

After a time, I no longer made any differentiation between God and true nature. After all, the sacred can only be one thing, right? The sacred can't be two things, true nature on the one hand and God or divinity on the other. But I wasn't making any attempt to conceptualize what God was, which might have been partly the influence of the Islamic teachings. In the Islamic faith, and somewhat similarly in the Hebraic faith, God is something you're not supposed to visualize and make a form of. You're not supposed to know God, you just believe there is God, and that's it. So that influence might have played a part in why I didn't try to think of God as something in particular or as a particular dimension.

Along with the thread of experiences that brought a feeling a nearness, of coming closer to something, I also had experiences similar to the one I described in chapter 5, of coming to a place of objective hopelessness and giving up. And I recognized that it is in the giving up that something happens, something that I call grace. The moment I gave up, it seemed that a certain energy descended and flowed into me, which turned out to be what I now call divine love. That energy simply melts the ego; it melts the self, and it melts whatever show of resistance the self puts up.

So I didn't really get to a place where I could think of divinity or being in any concrete way until I started having experiences of the boundless dimensions. It made sense to me then to experience essence not just as my nature but as the nature of everything, as a conscious presence that is alive and aware. It's not only the nature of everything and the essence of everything, it also constitutes everything, so nothing exists outside of it. That's what I came to call God, or divinity or the sacred, because inherent in the positive experience of boundlessness is the recognition that there can't be anything else apart from it. If you're experiencing unity, oneness, and boundlessness, it's logically impossible for anything else to exist.

So my mystical unfoldment, which began with a purely spiritual recognition of essence as presence, true nature, and being, did in a sense lead to some kind of religious experience and religious development. And historical studies of mysticism, and religion with its more personal relationship to a divinity, show that somehow one tends to emerge from the other. In the West, for instance, you can look at the traditions of Judaism, Christianity, and Islam, which all started out as religions but then developed mystical components. The Eastern traditions, conversely, all started out as mystical and then developed religious components, which came to involve devotion to a divinity. Even Buddhism has that nowadays—there is, you know, devotion to the Buddha, who represents true nature.

So it was through the objective understanding of the Diamond Approach that I came to see the relationship between these two sides of spiritual development: the religious approach with its personal relationship to the sacred, and the mystical approach involving the realization of inner nature. Now, a personal relationship to divinity is actually a natural and useful approach to the recognition of true nature and the realization of being. That it happens naturally is mostly due to what we talked about before—the depth, the tenacity, and the crystallization of the belief that there is the conventional physical world, where there is me and there is you as individuals. This belief is so deep that it's probably part of our phylogenetic programming. And this is why the mystical approach is not easy for most people, because it requires a perception of reality that is liberated from that belief, a recognition that essence, being, and true nature exist independently of the individual. From the mystical perspective it doesn't make sense for you as an individual to have a relationship to true nature, because you *are* true nature, you *are* being—it's all oneness and unity. But that's a very difficult perspective to reach, and although a few people manage to go through the mystical process—opening up and recognizing the unity and oneness of being—most people can't do it. Most human beings just can't transcend and let go of that deep belief, inherent in the ego principle, that they are separate individuals. And in order to deal with that difficulty, all spiritual approaches, even mystical ones, will at some point develop some kind of religious approach that involves the individual relating to the divinity.

In the Diamond Approach, the religious component arises when it comes to the transition between the personal, individual experience and the experience of boundlessness, pure being, or unity. That's where I see it as useful, and that's where my own experiences of a kind of religious feeling of devotion arose, a committed devotion to some kind of force that didn't feel like it was inside me. The notion of it being inside me wasn't relevant at that point. It was useful to my process that a devotional attitude to that force arose naturally and spontaneously, even though I wasn't normally oriented that way at all.

So my experiences gave me a sense and understanding of what a personal God—or a personal relationship to God—is.

A personal God does not mean God as a person; it means that you relate to God as if you are a person. There's a relationship between the person and beingness, a relationship between the soul and true nature. As a soul, as long as you still believe you are an individual, your relationship to being is bound to be personal. Because you believe you are a person, then of course your relationship to the sacred is a personal relationship. But it's *your* relationship that is personal, not God's. And it does not make the sacred a person—it just makes the relationship personal. We usually think a personal relationship has to be between one person and another person, but when we get to the transition from the personal dimension to the boundless dimension, we find that there can be a personal relationship between the person and the divinity that is not a person. So God does not have to become a person to relate to you personally or for you to have a personal relationship with God.

So I feel the word "God" should only be used when you're referring to a personal relationship to the sacred. If you're not, then there's no need for the word "God"; saying "true nature" or "reality" is enough. But for those who haven't had the experience, it's difficult to believe that there is such a thing as a personal relationship to true nature—that you can experience a personal relationship to reality in the sense that you love it, pray to it, and are devoted to it. But the fact that you can have such a relationship doesn't mean true nature is like a person that rewards or punishes you. It's this reward-and-punishment thing that never made sense to me at all. I could never believe that reality could be based on something as simplistic, primitive, and pedantic as a God of punishment and rewards.

Of course, a personal relationship exists from the beginning in our work, when it manifests as the love of truth. Loving the truth, having a total dedication to recognizing the truth and allowing it to open up and guide us—that is a personal relationship to essence, or true nature, and it's already implicitly a personal relationship to being and to the sacred. As the truth manifests as essential nature itself, and then as being as a whole—the nature of everything—the relationship develops more explicitly into a personal relationship to being, whether it appears as divine being, supreme being, or absolute being. Sometimes we simply use the term "the Beloved" to refer to this divine other since the relationship is characterized by profound love and devotion. When it comes to that level, it's easy to see it as a relationship between you and God, where the term "God" can be used to mean boundless beingness. So this personal relationship to being, or the sacred, experienced with the love and devotion that began as a devoted love of the truth, will continue in the Diamond Approach as long as you are a person.

However, at some point it's better not to use this language of personal relationship, because a subtle confusion can arise from it, and for most people there is a very real danger that the religious attitude can then become misguided. The danger is that when we are taking a personal relationship to the sacred instead of a more mystical one, we can become fixated as a subject relating to another object someplace else. So yes, it may happen naturally and serve a useful purpose that I find I am the soul relating to the divine, but it becomes a problem if I remain stuck in the dynamic of that object relation, because then I'm *always* the soul relating to the divine—whether it's essence, being, or divine being—and the divine *always* remains somewhere else. But we know from all the spiritual teachings with a mystical perspective that the fulfillment of self-realization is to *become* essence. I become the divine being, and I *am* true nature, I am the absolute. That is the true liberation.

We cannot arrive at this ultimate self-realization if we remain stuck in that usual kind of object relation with the divine. And that's likely to happen if we do not take into consideration one of the major insights of object relations theory, championed by Otto Kernberg. As we normally understand it, an object relation is between you as the subject and the object, right? You internalize that object relation, and in doing so you become the self that is relating to the object. But Kernberg's great insight was that the experience doesn't only consist of that dynamic—it can also be flipped. He saw that an object relation can be experienced from both sides. This means that you can also identify with the object image, so you become the object and project the self onto somebody else and relate to them that way. If we recognize that fully, then that can actually help us deal with the personal relationship to the sacred, because without that other understanding of the object relation, it will always be you, the self, relating to the sacred. Then you can never become the sacred. You can never become essence and being. So Kernberg might not know it, but he might be the corrective. He might have brought in an idea that can help us deal with our religious attitude so that it doesn't become misguided.

In our work, we take the more mystical attitude for a long time before we introduce the personal element, to avoid this possibility of confusion. In a sense, we have to be grounded enough in the recognition of our own completely pure and sacred true nature before we introduce the question of a personal relationship to the sacred. As I said before, the personal relationship is there from the beginning, but we don't focus on it, we don't explicitly say that's what it is at that point. And that's because while there is value in dealing with the sacred from the personal perspective, another subtle difficulty that arises from it is that we identify as the person having the personal relationship. We take ourselves to be that person, and we believe it completely.

Now, on the path of inquiry we start work from where we are and we allow that to unfold. That's what we always do in our work, because it's useful and efficient for the process of transformation to start from where we are. And since where you are at the start is in the entrenched belief that you are an independent, separate person, then we say okay, if that's what you believe, let's start from there. Let's take it as if it's true and go with it. And if that's what you believe, then when you recognize that there is a sacred reality, it's natural that you will relate to it in a devotional, humble, surrendering way. Taking this religious attitude, with its personal element, means that the spiritual impulse will appear from within the entity of the personality as a devoted and loving attitude toward the truth, toward reality. And this also then makes it possible for the belief in being a person to begin to dissolve. It makes it easier for the individual identification to come nearer to the unity through a process of attraction that is felt as love, until it eventually self-destructs through the intense love that comes from within it.

The realization of true nature appears then as the individual soul giving itself up, surrendering to or dissolving into a bigger reality that is pure and divine. And that dynamic seems to be intuitively easier for the identified part of us than just saying, "Okay, I recognize that I am true nature, so I will no longer experience myself as a separate person." Because even if you recognize your true nature in that way, the identification with being an entity, a person, will continue—it doesn't stop, just like that. We will explore this process of meeting the Beloved in much greater detail in the third book of this trilogy on spiritual love.

Now, I said right at the beginning, in chapter 1, that this language of surrendering is actually a trap, because in reality there is actually no one there to be doing the surrendering. In that chapter we explored the ultimate truth of boundless reality, but I also said then that at many stages of the journey it's pragmatic to talk of our process as one of "letting go," "surrendering," "melting," "disappearing," "merging," "uniting with." It may not be the ultimate truth, but it describes the truth of where we are at those stages, and that is what we're allowing for now as we look at our experience of the transition from the personal to the boundless.

As always in this teaching, it's important that we don't conceptualize what the truth is; we don't determine what this reality is that we are devoted to. That's why we simply say it's the truth and then let the truth reveal itself, whatever it happens to be, instead of saying from the beginning, "It's God," or "It's Brahman," or whatever religious concept you might choose. We can just leave it as the sacred, as divinity, as purity, as reality, and still be devoted to it in a personal way. And as the feeling of nearness grows, in time this reality, this underlying truth, will reveal its nature to the soul, and what it will reveal is that it is nothing but the soul's own nature.

So there is this process that takes the individual soul nearer to the divine being or true nature in a personal way, and we work through that personal relationship until it is gone, dissolved, leaving the experience of unity and boundlessness. In my own experience, that process was an inherent part of inquiring into the nature of the soul, the nature of being, and the relationship between the two. And what we've seen is that once we start to deal with that relationship, we have to deal with our unconscious personal relationship to God or the sacred. We started dealing with this personal relationship to the divine being in chapter 1, when we explored the personal experience of boundless love as living daylight. We saw that our capacity to feel basic trust depends on our early holding environment and how the relationship with the mother, or the mothering person, affects the relationship with God. We also looked at the issue of the beast, which can bring a hatred of divine love when the personal experience of it becomes frustrated.

I think it's inevitable for the psyche or soul to develop an image of a deity, or the sacred, even in people who grow up in mystical traditions such as Buddhism and Hinduism. It's because of a property inherent in the soul that makes it tend to personalize things. It's an unconscious tendency, and it happens naturally in children, so I'm sure that when Buddhist kids hear about true nature as the buddha nature, they can't help but make it into some kind of person who exists in some place. And then they will have a personal relationship to it. And where there's an image of a deity, there's usually an image of the devil too, so the beast will also exist in some form for Buddhists. Maybe it will look different from our images, but there will be something like that.

So almost everyone develops an image of God, and what's needed is to go beyond it and find out more about the relationship of the person, the human being, to the boundless being. Because the moment you see that even though there's boundlessness, you continue to be a human being and so does everybody else, the question arises: What's the relationship between the two? The dimension of Divine Love helps us to see clearly what the individual soul is, what cosmic reality is, and the nature of the relationship between the two. It helps make sense of humanity, of a human life and human relationships.

When we know cosmic reality, we see that being is the very nature of the soul. However, there is more that we need to understand about the relationship between being and the soul, because the soul is more than just its nature. It is an individual manifestation that is creative in a certain way. The soul is not the same thing as a rock, meaning it is not simply the ego self.

So there's more to learn, but one thing I hope we're clear about now is that when I talk about a relationship with the divine being, I don't mean the God that your mother and father or your priest might have told you about. As I said, I mean it in a very specific way. But what you need to do as I talk about true nature or divine being is to avoid conceptualizing it, to quit thinking you know what it is. Don't get ideas about what true nature is and how this bigger reality might manifest and appear to you as an individual. Just accept that you don't know what it is or what its relationship to you is, instead of constantly trying to imagine, "What is it? What's it like? Is it above me up there, and I am down here? Or am I inside it?" You need to let go of any ideas you might have about how it all works and go on a journey of discovery. For me it was through such a process of discovery that I came to realize what divine being is. It began with the story of Jabba the Hutt and transformed Jabba the Hutt into the son of God. We will explore what this means in the next chapter.

PRACTICE SESSION
YOUR EXPERIENCE OF GOD

• • •

Now is the time for you to explore the history of your relationship with God. Even if you feel you don't believe in God or have not been religious in your life, you may find you carry an unconscious feeling or experience of God. This will be a monologue, working with one or two other people if possible. Each person will take fifteen minutes to explore the following questions, while the others listen. Use any one of the questions as a starting point and follow where it takes you. If you are on your own, write out your answers.

> Did you have a religious upbringing? If so, was God an explicit part of your early life and your family environment, or was there a more implicit and unspoken notion of God in your upbringing? Were you more aware of God in the culture, or at your school, or in your social life with friends or neighbors?
>
> What was God for you—a presence, an idea, an image, a friend? What was your relationship to that God?
>
> How did your relationship with your mother and the quality of her holding impact your notion of God? Was the notion of God used as a means of control by your mother? Was God a refuge from difficulties at home?
>
> How has your relationship with God affected your spiritual journey throughout your life?

• • • • •

Questions and Comments

Student: I'm confused. When you experience yourself as a person and you have the devoted experience, and there's the feeling of nearness and love in your heart, I'm confused about the switch in that object relation, the one you talked about with reference to Kernberg. When would the switch happen? Can you explain that some more?

A. H. Almaas: So the switch happens as an experience I call self-realization. When you become what you're devoted to. You become the truth that you love.

S: So you're not really finding realization by being on the other side of the object relation. You're not really in an object relation at that point.

AH: There's the switch, where you become essential nature relating to the soul, to the individual.

S: The individual that you used to identify with.

AH: Yeah. You will see. So that's what I mean: The object relation switches. And by switching, you will become what you are devoted to. The nature of what you're devoted to is pure beingness, and that begins to dissolve the object relation. But it is possible to also experience yourself as the boundless divine nature loving the individual soul. So it is a relationship but not an internalized one.

S: Okay. Yes, I see.

AH: And then, of course, there is an art and a science of how to go from one to the other. That's the trick that needs to be learned, and I think it's a difficult thing for most people. It's like, when is the personal attitude useful and when is the mystical attitude useful? Because okay, you become true nature, right? But does that then mean you will never again be the person who is devoted to reality in a personal way? No. What will happen is that whether you like it or not, you're going to remain a person, because there's always an even deeper identification with being that person. So the skill you need to develop is this: The moment you recognize you're identified as a person, the best approach to take is one of personal, devoted love of true reality—you don't say, "I am true reality." When you're taking yourself to be a person, you don't say, "My true nature is Buddha." If you do that, you're lying to yourself. It will be a shell saying, "I am God."

If you're identified with being a person, you recognize that you are that person, and from there you take the personal attitude of having a loving devotion to the truth, without saying what the truth is. And then the moment that begins to switch and you become the truth, you drop that. You then work on not identifying with the person. Being as you are at that point, as the truth, you don't want to continue identifying with the person. If you do, that will take you right back into an object relation, which is not the truth, not the ultimate truth. The ultimate truth is that there's no object relation. The object relation is only useful because of our limitations.

That's the subtle art that needs to happen. When you are an individual, you have a devoted, loving prayerful attitude toward the truth. The moment you become the truth, you need to acknowledge it: "I am the truth. I am the light. I am the true reality. I am here. I exist. I am the ultimate." If you continue to think of yourself as a person, that will disconnect you from that.

However, there is an important exception, which is that you can be a person of being rather than a person based on ideas and history. This is when essential presence takes on the quality of personhood, but it's not a separate person now, because the person is an expression of the same substance as being, or divine love. Being this essential person means that you feel you are a wave that is a part of the ocean of love or a cell in the cosmic body. So you are not separate from the substance of the ocean or from the other cells.

S: What about when there's both sides? I'm thinking of some of Rumi's poems where he says, "I'm longing for you so much." And the answer is, "Quit complaining. I'm closer than your breath." And Rumi goes, "But I am only a single flame and you're the whole exquisite sun." So it's like the dialogue goes back and forth.

AH: That's right. It's a dialogue.

NINE

The Son of God

So far we've looked at the relationship to the sacred, or divinity, by focusing on the relationship with mother. That's because mother is usually the central figure in our early holding environment, and so our relationship with her largely determines our first fundamental experience of holding. The impression this leaves will affect our relationship to other fundamental experiences of holding, and above all, to reality, to the divine love that holds us. However, as we explore our relationship to God, or to our image of God, we find that this image has elements of both mother and father in it, so we're going to look now at how your relationship with your father affects your relationship to divinity. The relationship with father comes later—when you are more of a person—than the earlier, more primitive relationship with mother. And that's why it becomes relevant here, as we deal with you as a person in relationship to the truth.

I'll tell you about my own personal story and the experiences I went through in exploring this relationship. This came after the episode I described in chapter 6, when the experience of boundless divine love revealed my identification with the contraction in my body, which I felt as a shell. This led to the image of Jabba the Hutt as a dimension of that shell, which I then saw to be continuous with the cosmic shell. And finally there was the arising of divine reality, a divine presence that is love and light, and the recognition that I am an expression of this divine love, a part of the divine presence.

Now I want to go back to a particular point in that process, when I recognize myself to be part of this whole ocean of love. As this happens, I also become aware of my identity with the personal shell and with the cosmic shell, which is where I want to begin. As the cosmic shell, I feel one with physical reality. I feel I am part of the physical universe, just as a rock is part of a mountain. At the same time, divine love is present, but now it is only intuition rather than direct perception that tells me that it is the essence of the universe. I'd had the direct perception of this earlier, at which point there was nothing but the awareness of the love that is like an ocean of flawless presence. But here I'm aware of both the cosmic shell—the sense of the whole physical universe being just a dead, empty shell—and the cosmic divine being at the same time. Then I become aware that my identification is more with the shell, particularly the shell around the left side of my body. This is part of what I call the ego line of tension, which is the physical manifestation of the contraction in consciousness that comes with the formation of the ego structure and the belief in being a separate individual. The tension increases and can be felt all around my shoulder and chest. It's like some kind of shield, some kind of boundary around my chest.

As I experience that and stay with it, I become aware again of the divine love. With both present, at some point my identity shifts toward the divine love. When that happens, the shell begins to dissolve, revealing the image or identification that was inside it (the shell always has in it an identification of one form or another). The shield reveals the image of a young boy; it's the young boy I used to know myself as. This boy appears to me now, scared and holding tenaciously onto his mother's apron. This identification has emerged as I've become the divine experience of myself—the love that has no boundaries, with a quality of fullness and generosity.

So what's happened here is that the object relation has shifted. It's flipped in the way we discussed in the previous chapter. I've become the love, the divine presence, and from here I'm seeing this person, the Hameed that I have known from when he was young. The love that I'm experiencing begins to manifest a green quality; it is divine love with compassion for this scared young boy, who I see is not only scared but anxious and frustrated. I see his suffering, and I understand him. There is no rejection of him. From the perspective of divine being I am looking at this person, this identity that appears as a young boy, and the feeling that arises is, "You're fine, just as you are. You are welcome to stay. You don't have to dissolve; you don't have to die; you don't have to do anything. As boundless love, I love you and accept you just as you are. I can see your fear and frustration, and I understand your pain; I understand your suffering." This is what happens when you are identified with true nature and look at a person. You can't help but feel love and compassion because that is the nature of our essence.

So there's a feeling of being a person. And we've been talking about how the person dissolves and becomes a unity. That's the process, right? Some of us might therefore take this to mean that the sense of being a person is something we need to get rid of. But there's a feeling of rejection in that, which means we're still engaged in an object relation, one of rejection. Divine love, however, shows us that there's no need for rejection. There is nothing saying the person should disappear; the person is welcome to stay.

Although I feel the person is welcome to stay, at the same time a perception arises that shows this person, this boy, to be just an image, based on his belief that he is an individual. So we can see here how the object relation begins to dissolve naturally the moment you shift to the other side of it. But then, while I'm seeing that it is just an image, the contraction returns in my chest, but this time with a feeling of rage and anger. The boy is not just scared now; he's angry and full of rage. So then begins an oscillation of identity between the divine and the individual. The divine loves the individual, with all his difficulties and deficiencies, but the individual boy is angry at the divine because he felt abandoned by it during difficult times.

In this experience, the dynamic of the personal relationship with the divine becomes more apparent. As I move from the personal to the divine, there is the feeling of the divine loving the individual. But from the perspective of the individual, the anger and rage reflects a different part of the object relation. I recognize the boy's feelings to be part of the inner structure we discussed previously, called the beast, with its hatred of the divine. It says, "I'm really mad at you. I'm angry—where have you been all this time? You weren't there, especially when I was having difficulties." I can also feel that connected to the anger is a felt memory of my parents' suffering and their own feeling of being abandoned by God.

So there is this oscillation, a going back and forth between the two sides of the object relation with the divine. As this is happening, what comes to mind is my father's love for me when I was this little boy and how deeply hurt and angry at God he was. I'm seeing and feeling the hurt and anger my father had when I was around two years old; I think I was twenty months old when I got polio. Of course, both my parents were having a hard time of it—I almost died. They were scared, although it turned out that the polio only affected one leg. And what I recognize is that when my father was feeling hurt, angry, and abandoned by God during this time, I identified with him. And I see that my anger and frustration toward the divine has come from this identification with my father. My parents' feelings became mine through an identification with their suffering, and I learned from them how to feel about it.

As I see this, I feel a reawakening of the love relationship with my father. This was the first time in my process that I remembered his love toward me so explicitly. Before that, I knew he cared for me, but I didn't actually see and feel the love—it had become somewhat diluted in my memory. Here, I remember very distinctly seeing and feeling once again the passionate pink love that I had experienced from my father as a child, and I could see and understand his hurt and disappointment and his anger at God. So this rekindling of the love between my father and me came through exploring the relationship between me and the divine. Because when I became the divine and felt the love of the divine for the individual little boy that was me, it reminded me that my father also loved me just like that.

The next morning brings a state of happiness that continues for most of the day, though there is an ache in my neck and legs.

In the afternoon I see that I am not feeling a sense of identity anymore; I just feel empty. I feel I am an emptiness, or more accurately, I am nothing. Before, there'd been the switching from one identity to the other, but now all sense of identity begins to dissolve, leaving me with this feeling that I am nothing. But I also have more understanding of this process through having recognized the object relation between me and my father. Because of that, I see how my father's relationship to God has affected my own relationship to anything that comes close to being called God, or divine.

And now I can feel the sense of an essential diamond in the background, a stupa diamond. In the Diamond Approach, we explore the relationship between love and boundlessness through what we call the stupa diamond vehicle, which challenges and transcends the soul's deep belief that separating ego boundaries are necessary to feel unique and individual. The emergence of an essential diamond basically means that an essential quality arises in a way that brings precise, objective insight. By late afternoon I feel that this stupa diamond, which is silver, has permeated my being. This means that the aspect of personal will is appearing as will that has the precision of insight and the clarity of direct knowing, and I can feel the density, the hardness, and the fullness of it. It feels similar to the will of individuality but without the effort of individuality. The fact that this sense of true will arises as the object relation dissolves shows that the object relation had some kind of willfulness in it.

By evening I am questioning the desire for my individuality to disappear. Since I've been experiencing the divine, of course my desire for the divine has grown and with it the desire to stop being this separate individual. That's what I've been feeling: "I'm tired of being an individual. I've had enough. I don't want to be anymore, I just want to disappear." But as this will to disappear arises now, I'm beginning to question it, because I cannot see how I can be and function in the world if I am not an individual.

And then the insight of the silver stupa diamond surfaces in a way that surprises me. I thought that my true will would be to want to disappear, but the feeling that comes, with a sense of calm, is, "I accept the will of the divine, whatever it is." This shows a real understanding of true will, and I see the surrender it brings. I don't say what I want; I say, "Whatever is, if that's what the divine being wants, then that is what I want to happen."

As I'm lying in bed in the evening, paying attention to my experience, I feel the fullness of the pearly diamond, which is the personal essence with a diamond kind of precision. But on the surface I still feel a state of emptiness that I do not understand. The pearly diamond is a diamond manifestation of essence that brings an understanding of what it means to be a true person, but here there is just this emptiness, and when I feel the emptiness, I feel no sense of individuality. There's nothing unusual or striking about the feeling—it's almost bland. But then I realize that there is in fact a sense of individuality there—it's just very subtle. It's similar to ego individuality, but it doesn't have any sense of contraction or boundaries. This subtle individuality is a fullness that encompasses all of my body and also goes beyond it. For a while this does not make sense. Then I notice that my neck and legs are not aching anymore. My lower body, and my legs in particular, feel soft and warm. The ache in them has gone, and in its place there is this fullness that has a sweetness in it, a gentleness and a softness. And then I realize that they are full of divine light.

So now I experience myself as an individual rooted in the divine. It's not only that there is no sense of boundaries, there is no separation between me and the divine. I am just a wave in the divine ocean. This reveals the real personal relationship to boundless divine presence. When I feel the fullness of my personal essence, I feel that my individuality is continuous with the cosmic divine. When I feel the divine in the depth of me, in my lower half, in the belly center, I feel I am the infinite and omnipresent divine. If I feel it in the chest, in the heart center, I become this pearly presence that is an extension or continuation of the divine. And so there is the recognition of what I am: the son of God.

What does that mean, "the son of God"? It has a specific meaning in the Diamond Approach, and it's not the usual sense of "the offspring of," as the child of the mother and father that gave birth to us. If I say I am the son of God, it doesn't mean that I am here, God is somewhere else, and he gave birth to me. It means giving birth to me in the sense that it is my ground— it's what constitutes me. It means that the divine, the God presence, is here, and out of this God presence something individual emerges, something personal. And that is the person that I recognize myself as at this point, while recognizing that I am both this person and God at the same time.

There has been much theological discussion about the incarnation of Jesus Christ and what it means when he is referred to as the son of God. Some people say, well, it just refers to a human being having a divine spirit. And other people say, no, he really is God incarnate because he is of the same nature as God. I don't know whether my experience addresses those questions, but what it shows me is that to be the son of God is to recognize that I am indeed of the same nature as God. I am God, but God appearing as an individual amongst individuals, while still being this boundless presence at the same time. It's like a mountain on Earth. A mountain is a part of Earth, and in that sense you could say that the mountain is "the son of Earth."

So I am both the infinite and the individual. And this makes sense of the process I've been through in coming to understand my personal relationship to the divine. It began with experiencing my ego individuality as the contraction and tension of the ego line around the body. This can be as strong as a brick, and in me it manifested psychologically as a man who feels strong and is angry at God. Underneath that object relation was another one—a scared young boy who loves his father and models himself on him. Seeing and feeling the love of the divine for the individual brought out the love between father and son, and this dissolved the ego individuality. The silver stupa diamond then emerged, with a state of surrender to divine will. This allows the personal essence, the pearl, to appear, the true individual who is connected to the divine ocean as a manifestation of it.

This state is an experience of fullness grounded in divine being, with a mind that is empty and clear and full of diamonds. A pearl with its center connected to the divine and a lower body rooted in the boundless. The feeling is "I am the divine person. I am the son of the divine."

It is this exploration of the personal relationship to the divine—including the object relations involved in it—that leads us to the true relationship between the individual soul and divine being or true nature. It is as if the love that is an infinite ocean coalesces in a certain location as a personal arising, a personal being, a pearl. Thus the individual soul is experienced as a particular incarnate manifestation of true nature.

So, I've given you an example of how my relationship with my father affected my personal relationship to the divine. Of course, the dynamics might not be the same with your father; there might be variations. That's something for you to explore.

PRACTICE SESSION
YOUR RELATIONSHIP WITH GOD
· · ·

So now there is an opportunity for you to look at your own personal relationship to God and how your relationship with your father has affected it. This will be a fifteen-minute monologue, but during the monologue you will explore two different perspectives on the relationship—your own and God's. Work with a partner or in a group of three if possible. If you are on your own, you can write down your exploration instead.

In your monologue, consider how you feel about God, the divine, or true nature. Talk to the sacred and notice what feelings arise—maybe you feel angry, hurt, blessed, grateful, puzzled. Maybe you feel close to it or totally distant from it. At some point consider how it would be to see the relationship from God's point of view. What would the divine being have to say to you? How would it describe the connection you two have? See what happens if you speak for the divine. Again, notice what the feeling is when you talk from there. If there's time, you may want to keep changing perspective so it becomes a dialogue.

Afterward, you and your partners can take ten minutes to reflect together on the two or three explorations. If you are working alone, reflect on your own monologue. Can you see how your personal relationship to the divine may have revealed the object relations that are involved in it? Did it specifically reflect anything about the experience of your relationship with your father? Has the love relationship with your father, or the absence of it, affected your love relationship with the sacred?

· · · · ·

Questions and Comments

Student: I'm feeling very disturbed, and I need your help in making a discrimination. Because the way I've understood it in the past, when I've dialogued with what felt like my higher self or my guidance directly, talking to it, my experience was that in a sense, God was talking to me. I would feel a divine presence. I would feel a profound trust. I would feel a kind of melting and surrender, as if I was in the presence of the divine. And so I'm still not clear—I have the sense that sometimes you could talk to God and it would be an object relation, and you'd be talking to your father, or you'd be talking to your mother. But sometimes you actually do talk to whatever little opening you have of contact with the godhead, whatever it is. It speaks through you, and it could guide you in your life, quietly, or you could actually have some sense of talking to it. So for me there's a real discrimination between being in the presence of the divine and talking to the divine, however that miracle happens, and having a dialogue with the object relations that you've projected onto it. And I just need more help with that, because I got very agitated doing this exercise, because I feel like I *can* talk to a divine presence. And it isn't my father or my mother. Or I could talk to my projection onto the divine. So now I'm worried that I'm deluded and I need reassurance.

A. H. Almaas: What you say is true. You can have some kind of relationship with the divine in the sense that there is a dialogue.

Or that could in fact be an object-relation dialogue. Most of the time it's a mixture, just like with anything else. So in the way we were doing it, the aim was to clarify that object relation through the back and forth and find out what's involved in it. So that in time the dialogue you might have will be more of a real dialogue, and there will be less and less of the object relation in it. And we'll find that as there is less and less object relation, after a while the dialogue will become more of a monologue. There's no two then, at some point. As long as there's two, there is some kind of object relation.

S: Well, that brings in the other part. My guidance has been telling me for years now, and it came into full focus last summer, that it was time to stop dialoguing and it was time to be the guidance. And so I've actually stopped doing the dialogue, and I've been trying to sense moments when I am that. And somehow I felt maybe I misunderstood you and that you felt that wasn't the way or that wasn't a good thing to do.

AH: No. I think you should continue following that guidance, but you don't have to be completely rigid such that when there is an opportunity to learn something from a dialogue, you don't take it. Guidance is never rigid. Guidance can tell you it's better to do it that way, but once in a while you might not.

S: It felt like a real dependency, an addiction I've been trying to let go of . . .

AH: Yes, it might be, so it's good, what you've been doing. You should continue with that. But I'm saying that if you start experiencing yourself as a person, there are two ways to work: You could explore the person, your identification, right? Or you could do a dialogue with the person, until the dialogue fuses.

S: Okay. I understand better. Thank you.

S: I had an interesting experience of going very deep. I went last of the three, and I felt that when I was God talking to me, I couldn't see myself. So my usual experience of God is that he's not there, but when I was speaking for the divine, I felt more magnanimous and huge. So I would say, "I am here, and everything you have, you have got from me." Because it's felt like a struggle most of my life, that *I've* had to do it. And I haven't had God to help me. I've been on my own.

AH: Right.

S: And then as I continued, I realized that I have been served by God. And toward the end, I found that as I spoke as the divine, the answers to my own questions came very quickly. And then the answers weren't necessary. And then even the questions weren't necessary. So I felt a real blending of that, you know, a lot of energy in my body and it wasn't necessary to have the two perspectives any more, in a sort of affirmation that I really have been served in my life by guidance. And that in some way I was fighting against acknowledging that.

AH: So it's a good recognition. That's an interesting thing, when you do an exercise like this and the exercise actually works. It sort of diffuses itself, so you start with two perspectives on the relationship, but as it really starts working, after a while, the duality of those perspectives might not feel relevant any more. And you will see as we go on with this process of working with the personal relationship with God that you do the process, but then the process diffuses itself. And the part you started with begins to become unnecessary.

S: I had a very moving experience. For me, God the object was . . . I quickly got the impression that it was not caring, either couldn't or maybe didn't want to light up my world and had no interest in warming my world. It actually had a positive intention, but it was really passive and self-centered and didn't want to do anything. Didn't really want the job of being God. And I saw that I spend a lot of my time going around in my world—I had the image of lighting candles and lanterns—trying to warm my world up and light it, and that there is a real futility in that process. It takes so much energy to try and do that. And at that point, realizing that God the object didn't want to be there and couldn't be there, I felt this incredible relief. Like I didn't need to bang on that door anymore and try and get it from him. And, in a way, I have been keeping my world grey in the hopes that he would light it up and warm it up. And so, in the sense of relief, then it was like, well now what do I do? Lighting these lanterns and candles doesn't do it. Looking for God to do it, God the object to do it, doesn't do it. And what I felt at that moment was there was nothing to do but simply be it. That I could just let it radiate out from inside me. And even what I've been doing, in a way, with this work—trying to remember to be present and in the moment and notice the flowers and really kind of working to be present—was another kind of lighting the candle and the lanterns, trying to get something. And this was a different place of just really being and not having to do anything.

AH: So that's it. There are two ways, usually, that you could arrive at the realization: by going inward or through a personal relationship that diffuses. People lean one way or the other. In our work we mostly do it through self-realization, but we introduce the personal part as an element that helps deal with some of that identification.

S: What this kind of did was just . . . it was a very difficult exercise. It felt like you were asking us to do two opposite things: talk to something that's impossible to conceptualize—God—and then also talk to an internalized reality, the father. What kept coming up for me was more reason to doubt the existence of God. But because of the third part of the question, which was how does this reflect my relationship to my father, and it's like they both feel like enneagram fives. They're both so withholding. And when I became . . . you smile . . .

AH: It was just funny that God is fixated.

S: I'll unfixate him then. But in my experience in doing the exercise the right way, I just kept this parallel. And then it kept coming up around my father, who's very withholding and implosive. And he wouldn't . . . he had a very difficult time. I didn't even know who he was. So when I was God, when I became God, it was exhilarating. And the person who gave me the feedback also pointed out that it was very caustic, as when I was God talking to me, I said to myself, "You're going to have to work your ass off to get to know me. And to get to see me. And to get to feel me." And that's the work I'm doing with my private teacher, that I'm afraid if I go really deep, there won't be a spiritual self. I know that's an identification with my father. But the person who gave me feedback was reassuring because she said, "My sense is you really want to find God." And I think I really do. But he's so hard to trust. And he's so elusive. I just relate to that which is tangible. So, I guess that's part of my work—to allow for the elusiveness and trust in the elusiveness.

AH: Yeah. And it's good that you saw how the relationship with your father gets in there, when you explore your relationship with the sacred. That's what happens for everybody, you can't help it.

S: The problem in my inquiry was that I couldn't speak for God. I started to talk in the exercise, and as I was talking I realized that talking to God was like talking to my father. And my father provided shelter and food and clothing, but he wasn't available. And what came up for me is the night shortly after my mother died. I spoke to my father on the phone. He was living far away, and I told him I really wanted to get to know him. That with my mother not being around, we'd finally have an opportunity, maybe, to love each other. And he died that night. And I don't know if I think God is dead, or if I just won't be able to get to some . . . Ohhh . . . I'm afraid I think God is dead, and there's nobody out there. And the only thing that I have gotten, if there is a God out there, is the same thing that my father gave me when I was a kid: shelter and money and, you know, cars. But I don't have a connection. I don't feel the connection. I keep coming here, hopefully, to find the connection or to find the way for the connection. I think deep down I really don't believe there's a God out there, or if God is there, he's dead, like my father, and I won't have the connection with him.

AH: I didn't know whether there was a God out there or not. But I felt, if the truth is out there, I'm going to find it. Just find out. You don't need to believe anything. We don't work with belief. Some people say the truth is out there, instead of in here.

S: There were a couple of things that were surprises for me. Well, as far as my father is concerned, he was very sweet. He was not very available, but I loved him very much. And I think he loved me too. And when I spoke to myself as God, it surprised me that God seemed to be a lot more expansive, warm, contactful, and available than my father was. It's also true that God has been considerably more those things than my father was. And the other thing that was surprising was that I noticed that I seemed to separate from the past. I noticed that God as the divine seemed very formless, very radiant, and very loving. Manifestation, on the other hand, which seemed quite separate, is very iffy in my experience. Doesn't necessarily like me. But when I look back over my shoulder, there's every evidence in my life that everything wonderful has been provided in abundance. But I don't see it in the moment. It's only looking back that I see it.

AH: Well, maybe one thing you could do is, you could look from there. See what happens.

TEN

Surrender

One of the spiritual teachers who understood both the personal and nonpersonal perspectives of spiritual work was Ramakrishna. Although he was familiar with the mystical path of God-realization through self-annihilation, for much of his life he preferred a more personal, religious approach. He explained this by saying, "I don't want to be sugar. I want to taste sugar." With the mystical approach you become reality—you are divinity, you are the sacred, you are essential nature. With the personal approach, it's more a question of you having a connection with the sacred, feeling yourself to be in contact with it and tasting it. Our approach here is mostly the mystical path of self-realization, but we do see a place for the personal approach. We've seen how it can usefully complement the mystical approach, making the path of self-realization more possible and effective. So there are many facets to the Diamond Approach and many elements in our work. Sometimes our approach is one of very precise, epistemological discrimination. At other times we can be devotional and work with an attitude of ecstatic abandon, with ecstatic chanting or singing. Sometimes our inquiry is playful, and this playful inquiry can bypass the intellect and have direct impact, the way Zen practices do. We will see all these different approaches as we go through the boundless dimensions; each one of them has a different flavor, a different quality.

In exploring the boundless dimension of Divine Love, for the most part we've been taking the mystical approach to self-realization. So we know this is one side of our work: We explore our experience in our soul, we find out what our true nature is, and this true nature becomes our very identity. We are, then, essential nature; we are divine love; we are the supreme being. But there is then another side to our work: to bring that true nature into the world as a human being. And that's the side we call personalization. It happens in our work with all the aspects and in all the dimensions. With each aspect, first you experience it and realize it in your own soul, and then the challenge is how to embody it in the world. And as you continue to work on recognizing your identifications, you go through the empty shell, which leads to self-realization when you fully recognize that true nature is what you are. And then this other process happens, where that true nature becomes personalized as you embody it in the world as a human being. So these two facets— self-realization and personalization—occur on all levels of our work, on the personal level and in each of the boundless dimensions. The personalization process is part of what we call actualization of realization.

It might seem paradoxical that the initial process of working to liberate ourselves at the personal level—freeing ourselves from our object relations and our personal relationship to the divine—ultimately leads to the personalization of our realization. But this is now a different kind of personhood, when the beingness that is our true nature becomes a person in the world *without* the loss of its inner identity with true being. This is what makes self-realization relevant for humanity, relevant for human beings living a normal life. And that is our approach, to live a normal life. It's no accident that the Western traditions tend to value personal life more than the Eastern traditions, because the West places more emphasis on the personal approach to spiritualization.

So there is this evolution of our personal approach to being. First the relationship has a personal feeling of love for and connection with being. At some point there is a feeling of union. And then ultimately we become an extension of being, an individual expression of beingness. But remember what I said: Being is not one thing in particular. We're exploring it from the perspective of divine love at the moment, so we're calling it divine being. But that doesn't mean that every time we relate to or experience ourselves as being, well, that's the way it is, and there is no more to the divine or to being. Because being doesn't have an end in that way. It doesn't have a final form.

That's how the Sufis take the statement "God is greater." Many people understand the Islamic call to prayer, Allahu Akbar, to mean "God is great" or "God is the greatest." But a more accurate translation would be "God is greater," which expresses the idea that "God is greater than that which you have imagined." So the Sufis say, "Every time we experience God, we remember God is greater than that." There is no end to what God is, and so you never end, and that's why you should never constrain yourself. This Sufi sense of "God is greater" is the same thing as the openness of inquiry, where you never come to a conclusion. You see the truth, and you recognize the truth as what you are experiencing now, but your mind doesn't come into it and say, "Well that's it, the door is closed." Truth always has the possibility of expanding.

We should always remember that there are many dimensions of being, so it's possible in the Diamond Approach that we might first experience beingness as pure beingness. In my experience it first appeared as the divine being, and then I experienced it as the supreme being, then as the nameless being, then it became the absolute being, then it became the nondual being, and then it became the nonlocal being. Each one of them more mysterious than the last. By the time we get to the absolute being, we are already losing any possibility of a position about it. And when in time we get to nonlocal being, the mind doesn't have anything to grasp on at all. That truly opens the unfoldment and allows it to be completely open-ended. Because being is endless, as Gurdjieff made clear when he called being "his endlessness." Instead of saying "his majesty," he said "his endlessness." There really is no end, you see. It's the same thing with the Kabbalistic Ain Soph. Some interpret it as "the infinite," but the literal meaning is "no end."

When we use the religious approach in an objective way as part of our unfoldment, as part of the inquiry of the individual soul addressing the truth, it is not a matter of a truth that is outside of the soul, that God is out there. To consider that the truth, sacred reality, or God is outside, or to wonder if the divine is inside, means that you're still believing in your separating boundaries. Truth is neither inside nor outside; it's both and neither. That's the truth of boundlessness—it means everywhere. And when we get all the way to nonlocality, we recognize that the question of *where* is irrelevant. The question of where the truth is, whether it's inside or outside, means you believe that space is ultimate to the truth, which it isn't. So when addressing or loving the truth, you don't think of it as outside you or inside you. You just devote yourself to the truth. That opens the door for the truth to reveal itself.

The heart of the religious approach is prayer. Traditionally this has meant kneeling, with palms together and bowing one's head. But prayer can take different forms, including chanting, invocation, and dance. What is essential is the attitude. As you pray, the prayer reveals the truth about the one that is praying—that as a separate individual, you are not the source of any goodness. The source of goodness is being itself, true nature itself. We've discussed before the question of where essence comes from—how some people might see it as coming from inside them, others as coming from outside. But it's really coming from the presence of being that is everywhere—whether we call it divine being, supreme being, or true nature.

As we pray, the attitude of prayer is one of humility, a relinquishment of arrogance, a relinquishment of pride, a letting go of willfulness, a letting go of the sense of "I know; I know what to do." It means accepting one's helplessness, recognizing "I can't do it by myself." Because it's true, the separate soul cannot. The separate soul gets all its qualities and goodness from essential nature. The moment we take ourselves to be a separate soul, we disconnect ourselves from our source, and then we're deficient. And prayer shows that; it exposes this inherent deficiency of the ego. So you're acknowledging that as you pray.

The belief that you are a separate entity can be seen as the original sin, the ultimate sin. And you could say that every attitude, every action we take that doesn't express our true nature can be called sinful. But that's the meaning of sin according to the Work, not according to traditional religion. According to traditional religion, sin means that you've done something against God, something bad, something wrong, and you should be punished for it. From the perspective of the Work, sinning means not expressing the truth, not expressing your true nature. It means being inauthentic, being fake, being false. It's when you're believing yourself to be something that's not true, and at some point you realize that you're experiencing yourself and acting in a way that doesn't express the truth of reality.

In prayer, the soul takes the attitude of humility, an objectively humble attitude that is taken with sincerity, praying to a reality that it knows is bigger than it and is the source of all possibility of nourishment, love, transformation, release, and redemption. Grace comes from true nature; acceptance comes from true nature; love comes from true nature; forgiveness comes from true nature; support comes from true nature. And we can put true nature outside—project it outside and pray to it as God as some people do—or we can see it as something within us, to be realized. In truth, it's in both places, because it's everywhere and is always one and indivisible.

That's the basis of why prayer works when you really engage in it. Prayer works when you begin to objectively recognize your position. As you pray, you recognize your situation and your helplessness more and more, and you recognize it in an emotional way that melts your heart. It involves a recognition that is like an unfoldment, unfolding you in just the same way that inquiry unfolds you. True objective prayer unfolds you until you see the truth. And the more you see the truth, the more you get into the prayer, and the more there is surrender from a very deep, heartfelt place.

We've also seen the importance of working out our object relations and the conditioned patterns of our personality as part of the personal, religious approach to the divine, as that too leads to the surrender of the person to the sacred truth. I described how seeing the love of the divine for the individual brings out the love between father and son, and it's the same with father and daughter. It can also happen the other way around—as you recognize the love between you and your father, then your relationship with the divine can become more loving. Either way this makes the individuality, the person, begin to dissolve. In my own experience, this brought out the silver stupa diamond, which brings a state of surrender to divine will. This allows the true individual, the personal essence, to appear with its feeling of connection to the divine ocean. Surrendering one's will to the divine liberates the true will, which forges the connection to the divine.

It's important to work out these object relations, between you and your mother and between you and your father, so that whatever imagined relationship you have to sacred reality, to the truth, or to God, the divine, true nature—whatever you call it—can be experienced as a relationship of trust, a relationship of love and surrender. The reason that's so important is that in order for the individual, the separate self, to let go, for it to dissolve and recognize its divine true nature, it first needs to surrender its will. And the personality, the individual, will not surrender its will easily. We know from experience that we only surrender our individual will when we recognize that we are personally loved by that which we are relating to. Otherwise, it's too difficult for us to trust and let go. So we have to feel personally loved by beingness, by our essential nature, by God, by the divine, by the truth. You need to feel it as a love for you, personally, before you can let go and surrender yourself to it.

And when you recognize that, yes, this nature that I love also loves me, then what's the point of resisting? What's the point of trying to hold on? What's the point of saying, "I have to use my will to get what I need"? You recognize that you're in good hands. And the fact that the individuality isn't trying to hold on allows grace to arise as divine love, which then melts the separateness and connects us to the divine. It's understandable that we don't really believe grace will arise for us or touch us if we don't believe the divine being loves us, because grace is love emanating from the divine being. Divine love is being's love, the love of true nature. If the individual is deluded about who and what it is, part of the delusion will be that true nature doesn't love this individual. So within that delusion, the individual needs to begin to feel that "I am being loved by this reality that I'm surrendering to." Otherwise, why surrender? And for us to be able to do that, we need to continue to work on and through our relationship with our parents, because that determines all our later relationships, including our relationship to God or true nature.

PRACTICE SESSION
SURRENDER AND SEPARATE WILL
• • •

In the following exercise you will explore your own experience around the question of surrendering your separate will. The exercise will be a monologue, so practice in groups of two or three, with each of you inquiring for fifteen minutes. If you are on your own, you can take fifteen minutes to write out your inquiry.

Consider the following questions and choose any one of them to begin your exploration. Be open to where it takes you as you follow the truth of your experience.

Do you believe that you need to use your own separate will to get what you need?

Do you have that belief with regard to finding spiritual fulfillment—that you need to use your individual will all the way along the path and that you have to liberate yourself?

Do your answers to these questions imply that you don't feel personally loved by being—that you believe you live in a world that's devoid of a loving God?

How do you feel about the prospect of giving in and surrendering? Do you believe that you will feel held? What else do you believe might happen?

• • • • •

Questions and Comments

Student: For me, it seems like the lack of the capacity to surrender my will is built right into me. It's part of who I take myself to be. It seems I have to leave for that to even happen. And there seems to be a rage and a tremendous sadness about that fact within the identity. And this, like, irrevocable attachment to the identity. Is it just a matter of hanging out with that attachment? Again and again and again . . .

A. H. Almaas: Yes. And understanding it. You're attached to it because you still don't understand that that's not the real you. So the more you understand that's not really you, that it's just a structure created by your mind, the easier it will be to let it go.

S: But the real me is so spacious, it's just . . . Maybe I'm experiencing the shell, but it just feels like an emptiness then.

AH: So, spacious, you say?

S: Yeah. Like what comes doesn't feel like it has any structure.

AH: Give it a chance to show you. God doesn't reveal the whole truth all at once, you know? Too much to reveal all at once. Spaciousness is needed first for new things to arise.

S: Okay. Thanks.

S: I am still a little or a lot puzzled with why father has to come in so much when it comes to God, what we call God. I could see every time when I experienced the infinite love that was God, then this father part would come in and it would reject or distance or whatever. And why is it father? It's a very narcissistic layer that feels like father, for me at least.

AH: Why is it father that comes in relationship to God?

S: Yeah.

AH: Don't really know for sure. First of all, we worked on the mother part, you know, your relationship with your mother, and the holding environment. So maybe that part is more worked out than the thing with your father. So the father is what comes up because it's still not finished. That's one possibility. Also in our tradition, the whole Western tradition, God is usually seen as the father, right? So it's in the culture, and maybe that cultural background can affect us to think of God more as father. That's possible too. So we could tend to project our father more on God than we tend to project our mother. Most people seem to alternate— sometimes father, sometimes mother—in relationship to reality.

S: You said earlier, also, "his endlessness." And so there's always this "his" and it's father.

AH: Yes. That's what Gurdjieff said: "his endlessness." Right.

S: It's sort of a little annoying in a way to me.

AH: It is?

S: Yeah.

AH: Right. Language, traditionally, has had it that way. That might make it easier. It disposes people to think of it that way, to have their father projected on ...

S: And I'm still curious if there's a deeper truth there in what father represents.

AH: That's interesting, yes. So, I'm sure that traditionalists will say yes. And if you talk to a real traditional Christian, they say of course, God is the father; it's masculine. Now, is that true or not? That's a good question. And I know in the Muslim tradition, God is not given a gender, right? However, when they do, they say "he." They say God is neither male nor female but they refer to God as "he" at the same time. They don't want to say "it" because God's supposed to be alive, so what do you do? Since it was men, I guess, who developed these things mostly, they say "he." But I think the more you get to the boundless dimensions, you'll see that both father and mother come up, really. And God is feminine, masculine, and neuter. But we've worked on the relationship with mother before, and we're focusing on the relationship with father now. That might be one reason why it might be coming up.

S: So father is not necessarily more connected to the boundless, or the barriers are more with father?

AH: Not necessarily, no. Father isn't necessarily always connected with the boundless dimension.

S: Thank you.

S: Could you please talk more about surrender? What I discovered is this angry, rejected part and that I have to surrender that. And it's as if I don't know how.

AH: You don't surrender that. It is that that needs to surrender. When you surrender, it means the person who says "No, fuck you," that's the person that at some point gets converted. That's the personal way of doing things, that's the religious approach. But the approach of self-realization, the mystical approach, is just to explore that part. And as you explore it, you see it's an image, and it begins to dissolve. So you let yourself feel angry and all that, and let that happen, let it unfold and understand it. Understand the relationship in it, let it work itself out.

I'll finish with a poem that I think expresses the sentiment that we need to see that divine love welcomes us and accepts us as we are, for us to be able to relax, to let go and feel held. It's called *Love*, by George Herbert, and it's from the beginning of the seventeenth century.

Love

Love bade me welcome: yet my soul drew back,
Guilty of dust and sin.
But quick-eyed love, observing me grow slack,
From my first entrance in,
Drew nearer to me, sweetly questioning
If I lacked anything.

"A guest," I answered, "Worthy to be here."
Love said, "You shall be he."
"I, the unkind, ungrateful? Ah, my dear,
I cannot look on thee."
Love took my hand, and smiling, did reply,
"Who made the eyes but I?"

"Truth, Lord; but I have marred them; let my shame
Go where it doth deserve."
"And know you not," says Love, "who bore the blame?"
"My dear, then I will serve."
"You must sit down," says Love, "and taste my meat."
So I did sit and eat.

ELEVEN

The Gift of Grace

W̲e've seen that Divine Love is the dimension of our true
nature that reveals the secrets of surrender. Learning
about divine love and realizing this way of experiencing being
can therefore help us understand something very important
about spiritual practice, the inner path, and the way we view in-
explicable things that happen in our lives—namely, the meaning
of grace, or blessing. I talked about the importance of grace in the
previous chapter, where we saw that we will only trust in grace if
we believe that the divine being is love or loves us. I want to focus
more now on the importance of understanding grace, because in
truth, it is not possible to comprehend how spiritual practices
work without knowing the action of grace. In other words, without grace, no practice can work. No liberation can happen without the gift of grace, without this loving action of true nature.
This is often not clear to us at the beginning of the path, and it
takes a great deal of experience and maturation to appreciate this
truth.

Many of the difficult things that happen in our lives are
also blessings in disguise. It often takes some time and some

understanding before we can see the grace in such happenings, because they can be painful, even traumatic. And I'm not saying that all traumatic experiences are blessings. Close observation does not show this to be true. But some are, and finding the right attitude toward such happenings is part of the grace. Our readiness to see the grace in them is also a grace, and that is often a result of the grace of our upbringing or circumstances.

So what is grace? What is blessing? It is simply the expression of being's love, the manifestation of divine love in the occurrences and experiences of our lives. Sometimes the grace is obvious. Frequently it is not, and it might take some time and work to see and appreciate it. So we'll end our exploration of the boundless dimension of Divine Love by discussing and exploring experientially its relation to grace, learning to recognize that we are always receiving its gifts, even when we are caught up in the representational world and those gifts are not immediately apparent to us.

In some sense the whole situation we have here is a gift—the opportunity for spiritual learning is a gift and what we learn is a gift. In my experience, this is true even though we may need to work very hard and exert ourselves totally in our practices. This is because exertion or effort is not what really does it in the end, even if it's often necessary for what does do it to be able to do it. Our practices can only take us so far. We can exert ourselves and walk with great determination through the desert to reach the oasis, but none of that will matter if the oasis doesn't actually show up when we get there. And that is not something we can make happen. The fact that things do happen that bring abundance, that bring freedom, that bring release—this is a gift. To illustrate this, I will tell you a few personal stories to give you my experience of how spiritual learning is a gift.

I begin at the time when I was a student, studying at UC Berkeley. I think I was about twenty-three or twenty-four years old, and at that time I was not really a spiritual kind of person. As I explained earlier, I wasn't interested in spiritual things at that age, and it's not that I had no interest, more that it just wasn't my concern. My focus was on what I was studying academically. I was very good at being a student, and I was very into it. Besides the classes and the studying, I was also into doing what students do—going to parties, having political discussions, going on dates, all that stuff. With some friends I used to sometimes go to this bar in Berkeley called the Steppenwolf. It was a dark and dingy place that was a popular hangout for students, professors, and artists—and more than a few acid heads. Everyone was into the writer Hermann Hesse at that time, which is why they liked the Steppenwolf bar—*Steppenwolf* being the title of one of his novels. The bar even had a sign over the entrance with a quote from the book: "For madmen only. Price of admission—your mind."

One night, a friend and I were walking out of the bar. It was around midnight, and we'd both had a couple of glasses of wine while hanging out and talking, but we weren't drunk. Our car was on the other side of the street, so we were crossing the street and talking and . . . that was the last thing I remember. The next thing I knew, I was lying in the street in a lot of pain. There was no one around—my friend wasn't there. A few minutes later an ambulance appeared. It turned out my friend had called it because there'd been an accident, which I seemed to have missed. The truth was that I was the one who had been hit, but without me knowing it. I really had no idea what had happened. I'd been walking along, I'd just said something to my friend and was waiting for his response, and then suddenly I was lying in the street.

And now I discovered that I was about half a block away from where we'd been standing.

At some point I understood that I'd been hit by a motorcycle, which neither of us had seen coming. I was in very bad shape, and I remember them putting me in the ambulance. That's the only time in my life that I've been inside an ambulance, and I remember I was in a funny kind of state. You might say I was in shock because I was alternately singing and crying—and neither of those are things I did much at that time of my life. People were trying to calm me down, and I remember I didn't know if I was feeling good or bad. But there was definitely a lot of pain. They took me to the hospital at UC Berkeley, where I was on the critical list for about three days and underwent several major operations.

The interesting thing is that even though the doctors weren't sure whether I would make it, I myself had no concern at all. In fact my only concern was how long this was all going to take and how long I would have to stay in the hospital. I wanted to get out as soon as possible. It was spring out there, and when I looked outside it was nice and sunny and at that time in Berkeley the flowers were so beautiful. I just wanted to get out. I *knew* I was going to get out—even if the doctors and nurses didn't know that—it was just a question of how long it would take. And from what I understand, my body healed very quickly, about three or four times faster than expected.

So I did get out fast, after three weeks or so. Normally, after a physical trauma like that you'd expect to be hospitalized for much longer and undergo all kinds of physiotherapy before being discharged. And the wisdom today is that you'd also need therapy to get over the psychological trauma. But in my case that didn't happen. In fact, most of the time I was in the hospital I was actually feeling happy and joyous. I ended up having to miss school for a whole year in order to fully recover from all the physical injuries, but one thing I never had to deal with was the expected state of shock. And I have yet to find the need to work with any shock or trauma from that accident—I've been looking for it ever since, but I've never found it.

It was only when my inner experience was unfolding a few years later that I recognized that what I was experiencing when I was in the hospital was basic trust. That when I looked outside and saw the sun, I was seeing living daylight. The whole atmosphere was pervaded with a sense of ease and lightness and a deep trust that everything was going to be okay. My feeling was, whatever happens is just right, and this feeling was accompanied by a sense of ease and relaxation. There was a feeling of being able to let go because of the sense that everything was being taken care of. And remember, this is despite the fact that up until then I hadn't had what people would call spiritual experiences—at least nothing that I recognized as a spiritual experience. Yes, I sometimes felt good or profoundly peaceful, but I didn't see this as something spiritual. It was only years later that I discovered the deeper nature of what was going on.

There are a few things about that accident that I didn't understand for some time. First of all, I didn't know what had happened between the time I was talking to my friend and the time I found myself lying on my back in the middle of the road, in pain from all the wounds and broken bones in my body. There was a gap in my memory of the experience. And the other thing I didn't understand was how I knew that I was going to be all right, even though the doctors weren't sure how bad the damage to the brain and other organs was. In fact, all the medical indications said there was a real possibility that I would die. It wasn't like I thought about the possibility of dying and felt I wasn't going to—the question didn't even come up for me.

It took some years before I regained the memory of that gap in my experience, and then I understood what was going on during that time and why I'd felt a lack of any concern. It was when I was discovering what we call in this teaching the diamond guidance. As I was learning to experience the diamond guidance in a full way—and then to be it—I started thinking about the accident and what had happened. And that brought up the full memory of it, which emerged as a reliving of the experience as if I was actually there.

It wasn't what I expected, and it wasn't what most people think happens during a traumatic experience like that. It was closer to what's called a near-death experience these days. What I remembered, or rather relived, was that as the motorcycle hit me, I was outside of the body. At the moment of impact, I experienced myself looking down at the street. I was seeing the motorcycle carrying a body—my body—down the street for half a block and depositing it on the road and then the motorcycle swerving with two people on it. It was totally peaceful as I looked down on the scene. That's what I remember: complete peace. It's like I was high up, and I could see the whole street—it was dark but I could see things very clearly. I could see that there weren't any cars around because it was very late at night.

Thinking about it now, I was probably clinically dead at that point. I didn't know that, and nobody could have known because there was nobody there until the ambulance came and my friend reappeared. So there I was looking down, and when I looked away from the street there was this vast night, a vast darkness. It was pure, luminous, and one hundred percent peaceful, and there was an ease and a total absence of any emotion whatsoever. Just complete freedom and complete peace with a sense that I could easily, happily, glide into that darkness. I felt drawn toward it.

While I was experiencing that darkness I was also aware of myself, and the interesting thing in that awareness was the recognition that I was a beautiful structure of diamonds. There were brilliant shining diamonds of different colors, making up a whole structure, a whole body, a whole design. That is what I later called the diamond guidance. So some kind of cognition and understanding was clearly possible from this place, but it was not the usual sense of thought. There was just knowingness—a knowingness of peace and a knowingness of how I felt, all while looking down and seeing that my body was in total pain. That's the interesting thing: I was looking into this darkness, this infinity of luminous beautiful peace, while also aware that the body was in total pain.

I looked this way and that way several times, my awareness shifting between the alluring luminous vastness and the body in all its pain. Then at some point, what arose when I looked at my body was intense love and joy. And as I experienced this love and joy, the pink diamond and the yellow diamond in this multicolored diamond-like structure glowed much more intensely—they radiated. And I realized that the love and joy, which are the affects of the radiance of the pink and yellow diamonds, had to do with the body, with life, with being on Earth. And it was this love and joy that became the force that made me happily, willingly, dive into my body. And then I was in great pain, and that's when I was singing and crying at the same time.

As I said, it was several years before I regained that part of the memory of the incident. And the interesting thing to see now is that, well, you couldn't really have a more intense shock to the system than this—with the kind of injuries that usually lead to great physical and psychological trauma—and yet it was at the same time a total gift, in some sense a complete blessing. Because this intensely painful experience did not create a traumatic effect. In fact it was the beginning of my awakening and in some sense therefore, the beginning of the teaching of the Diamond Approach. And as you see, I didn't do anything to make it happen. I wasn't practicing, I wasn't meditating, I wasn't doing anything. I was simply walking out of a bar.

I'm saying this partly to point out that having a difficult experience isn't necessarily a horrible thing that you just have to get over. That if we are open in a certain way, what we might think is a horrible experience can be an occasion of the greatest learning. It might be the most blessed moment of our lives for all we know. Now some people might say, "Well, probably if it had happened in childhood, it would have had more traumatic effects." But that wasn't the first major ordeal in my life. As you've heard, when I was a child of about a year and half, I had polio and almost died. But the results of that have not been traumatic either. Yes, I've had difficulties as a result of it—both physical and emotional— but I also see that this event has been another of the main blessings in my life.

I've related the story about the motorcycle accident to illustrate that when we talk about working on the realization of our spiritual nature, we need to remember that we're talking about a dimension that is already there. It's always there, even if we don't see it, and it is the source of all our experiences and all our realizations. And we've seen in our exploration of divine love that this source or dimension is by its very nature the essence of loving goodness. Its nature is to give, to bless us, and to offer us its abundance.

So these are examples of grace manifesting as blessings in disguise. I think when I was in the hospital, the body healed fast because of the presence of those blessings, which I experienced then as a kind of confidence, some kind of trust in reality. For me that was when I began experiencing the feeling of being taken care of, of feeling that there is goodness, there is abundance, and that things will be fine. I didn't think these things consciously then— it was more an unconscious sense that if we just relax, if we take things easy while doing the best we can, things will work out and usually in a much better way than we could have expected.

Again, I am not saying that all difficult experiences are grace or result in grace but that grace can happen even in such difficult situations. And I'm also not saying that the ever-present possibility of grace means that we ourselves don't need to do anything. It doesn't mean we can just waste our time, not make any effort, and not be impeccable. While grace can give us its blessings even when we are not engaged in any spiritual practice, as in my case, generally there is a dialogue or an interplay between our inner commitment to truth and our practices and the blessings of the spiritual dimension.

You've already heard from my journal entries about times when I was consciously working on certain issues with great intensity, doing my practices and paying constant attention to my process but experiencing great difficulties. I would often be feeling completely stuck and deeply frustrated that nothing seemed to be happening, even though I kept practicing and applying myself. It's an experience that many people report, this feeling that there is no progress at all. For me it has often come to the point where I've gotten so stuck, so frustrated, and so totally fed up that I finally give up. It's not out of anger at that point. In the end this giving up comes more out of a feeling of utter helplessness. It comes at the point when I truly recognize that I can't do it and that I simply don't know what to do any more.

Up until that point, I may think I know what do: "Ah yes, I'm being told to do this, this, and this. I understand." And so I do all those things, but nothing happens. And then I realize that deep down, I haven't got the vaguest idea, really. And it's only at those times when I really give up, when I recognize that I can't do it and I actually don't know how to do it, that something of a different order happens. That's when I feel some kind of release, some kind of letting go. But it's not really letting go—not in the way that people often talk about letting go, as if it's something that you can "do." It's more like I fully realize that I *can't* do it, and in that feeling there is a recognition of my helplessness, a feeling of my incapacity, my smallness, and my ignorance. And at that very moment something else happens. It's as if some kind of rain begins to fall inside, an inner rainfall that is gentle, delicate, soft, and sweet. And it is that delicate gentle rain that really dissolves the problem, dissolves the issue, dissolves the difficulty or the barrier. So I'm trying to make the point that besides recognizing the fact of grace, it's also important to recognize that there is a dynamic in it that relates to our inner practice—the process, and often the struggle, that comes before grace descends.

The exertion is not enough by itself then. But I do have to exert myself and do enough to reach the point where I recognize, "That's it. I've given it all I can and it doesn't work and there's nothing more I can do." I have to get to that point before I can quit the mental attitude that it's up to me. And it's not a technique. It's not like I can say, "Okay, so I have to quit trying to make it happen," because that's still thinking I can do something to make it happen. No, the trying just quits on its own with this recognition of objective helplessness, because the mental attitude that it's up to me also quits at the same time.

So those times when I've quit, it's only because I truly knew that I'd reached the end and there simply was nothing more that could be done. What else can you do then but quit? And it's in this state of utter helplessness that something manifests, something arises, something descends, something opens up. There's some kind of energy, some kind of presence or consciousness that arises and somehow melts me away. It melts the one who's having the problem, the one who's trying to do something about it.

Now, I've said before that the notion of the individual "surrendering" is only an approximation—that it's just an attempt to describe a process in a way that makes sense to us at certain stages of our journey. In truth, I wouldn't call it surrender. *I* couldn't surrender. I never surrendered, and no one ever surrenders. You see, to believe I'm surrendering means I still believe I can do something. But I can't let go. All that happens is I quit, and that's because I recognize that I can't do it. It's the grace, the blessing— it's that energy that does it. This dynamic has happened to me many, many times and that's how it's become clear to me that there is something else there that does it. There is a source, an energy, a presence, a consciousness—and that is what really does the work. It's only this that can bring about the release, and it's this that brings the resolution and the letting go.

So paradoxically, it's through such repeated experiences of failure that I've developed a kind of trust, some kind of faith, some kind of inner confidence in my process. It comes from a knowingness that it is not up to me. I'm not the one who does it; and if it wasn't for this other force, if it wasn't for this grace that can happen, I would never be released, and no development would happen. No true and lasting awakening can arise and no transformation is possible without this grace. And this has continued to be the major theme, the main thrust of my process. There came a time during some of the main discoveries of the Diamond Approach, such as the discovery of the aspects and the dimensions, when there was a complete trust that it's all happening on its own. And it's not only happening on its own, it's also pushing me and pulling me and showing me and releasing me and confronting me and melting me. This is one way grace works.

And it's interesting that what appeared to be a choice in the experience of the motorcycle accident—to go toward life and away from the nirvanic black vastness—was not really a choice. During that out-of-body experience, my usual self wasn't there to know what was happening and to make such a choice—my presence at that point was the diamond guidance, and it was that which guided me back to my earthly existence. That's why it's not surprising that once I'd returned to my usual sense of self, I couldn't remember what had happened. So there was no conscious awareness of the experience afterward, but the effect of it continued to be felt as an unconscious force. That showed immediately in the sense of ease and relaxation that came with the instinctive trust I felt in reality. The deeper effect became apparent as my life course changed several years later, when I realized that it wasn't physics that I wanted to study but the inner workings of the soul.

As I followed the destiny of that path—which eventually revealed itself as the path of the Diamond Approach—this unconscious force became more conscious and more powerful as my soul gradually became clarified. So it was only much later in life, when my soul had been clarified to the point where I could explore and fully be the diamond guidance, that I could know and understand what had happened briefly and spontaneously in that out-of-body experience.

At this later point, when my soul had become completely transparent—even empty of existence—especially around the heart, the heart then became a window through which I could clearly view the inner Beloved, the nirvanic luminous black vastness.* And looking through this clear window of the heart, I could see that the radiant and luminous darkness of the absolute is in the midst of earthly existence, because it is actually the true nature of the world. So I was now seeing and experiencing in a more developed way what I had seen during the accident. While I was out of my body I'd seen the dazzling luminous darkness everywhere. It was the space I was in, and it was darker and more mysterious as

---

* The motorcycle accident and its aftermath provide a striking illustration of the grace of divine love. The experience at the core of this incident, however, and the clarification of the soul described here, are manifestations of an even more subtle and fundamental dimension than Divine Love—the Absolute. On the journey through that dimension, the heart becomes empty of all its previous longings. It yearns only to disappear completely into the inner Beloved, the absolute source of existence, which manifests as the dazzling luminous black vastness referred to. Divine love is instrumental in this journey of the heart, for it is the source of the yearning for the Beloved, and it is the dynamic force that expresses the Beloved's pull on our consciousness. The mystery of this journey is the subject of the third volume of this series on love.

I looked outward. And yes, there was a love for that vast nirvanic darkness that I could have disappeared into, but there was also a love for human life, which brought out the love and joy of the diamond guidance I was experiencing as what I am. So the guidance simply took me back into the midst of life. I didn't have to leave life to find the peaceful darkness of the absolute—I found it by returning to life and following the terrain of the path of this teaching. And the teaching tells us that the path is not to leave this world; it is to be in the world but not of it. It is a path of embodied transcendence.

The experience had shown me briefly what I had been wanting all my life without even knowing it. From the very beginning, in some deep sense that was unnamed and unknown, I'd always felt in my heart that I was distant from something. And as I saw it again now, the dazzling luminous vastness in the heart of my clarified soul, I recognized more fully and consciously what I'd been wanting and that I didn't need to go somewhere else to find it—I was exactly where I ought to be. Here was where I recognized the source of all the blessing to be, the source of all the grace, all the luminous experiences, all the knowledge, and all the guidance.

This shifted my practice from never forgetting presence to never forgetting the source, which is a much subtler thing. It's a subtle art, how not to forget the source, because the source is not exactly presence—it's beyond presence. And again, in some sense it happens as a gift, when the source basically integrates the soul, integrates the life of the soul, so that the soul becomes the window or the vehicle for this mystery.

This process of grace working on my soul, from within and without, had begun with the work of experiencing the personality, and it then progressed—to experiencing the soul, to experiencing essence with all its aspects and dimensions, to experiencing being and its boundlessness, and then to experiencing the absolute, or the source. And the absolute, or the source, then integrates all of that experience into what I call the nondual absolute, which is basically experiencing myself as vastness, this vast mystery, in which all that we see in the world of appearance—people, trees, animals, cars, all objects—are now seen to be nothing but crystalline glimmerings within that vastness. Everything is like a multifaceted, multicolored clarity that is completely transparent to the vast luminous darkness. And when this luminous clarity that is everything manifests the sweetness of divine love, then it becomes clear that it is itself the blessing, it is itself the grace. Divine love reveals that true nature is the source of all grace—it is pure grace.

But what becomes important after a while is not these vast spaces and mysterious states of realization. What takes precedence is how to live in the world. The greatest gift is not that I recognize my nature as the absolute but in my being able to live in the world and act from that perspective of the absolute. The soul becomes transparent to the absolute, which then feels an intimacy with everything in the world. The focus for the soul then is not about experience but action. To really, truly, interact with other people and live in the world, with true sensitivity, with true intimacy. To be with somebody else and experience them deeply while leaving them completely alone, without the interference of any reactions, ideas, positions, hopes, or fears. And to be able to bring compassion, sensitivity, love, and intelligence to bear on such interactions so that the other person can also reveal that understanding of themselves. This again is the action of grace.

It's all a gift, you see. And it becomes a delicate, subtle matter at this point, because when you get to the boundless dimensions

and you experience yourself as presence itself, as true nature itself, it's possible to forget that it's a gift. Because you can start
to believe, "Well I am the source of everything." So how do you
keep that balance of recognizing that you are the source of everything while at the same time recognizing that everything
is a gift? Well, it's possible if the path remains based on what I
call basic trust. In Buddhism they call it trustful confidence. In
Christianity it's called faith. This basic trust or confidence always
involves a recognition of our limitations, our helplessness, while
at the same time informing us that just because we're helpless,
it doesn't mean it's the end of the world. It's not bad news. The
good news is that there is true nature, there is a reality that is a
source of guidance. It is a source that functions as guidance, and
the guidance is a function of grace, of blessing, which manifests
itself in the various experiences that happen and the knowledge
and realizations that come through them. And that blessing, that
grace, is the action of true nature. It's the loving action of true nature that makes it possible for the revelation of reality to happen.

The word I prefer to use for that grace, for that blessing, is the
Sufi word "baraka." It's more inclusive than the words "blessing"
or "grace." "Blessing" and "grace" tend to be used purely in spiritual contexts, so when people talk about grace it usually relates
to some kind of spiritual experience. The word "baraka" means
more than that. It comes from Arabic, and while it does mean
"spiritual grace," it can also mean "good fortune," "good luck,"
and "good influence." So it can be used in more material contexts,
such as describing your physical health and your life generally going right—getting the right kind of job, having the right kind of
relationship, and so on. But it also has to do with spiritual grace
in terms of the actual showering of blessings that brings about the

surrender and transformation. It can be experienced as a specific act of blessing or more generally in the overall sense of the optimizing force that enables our process to unfold. The optimizing force is how being expresses its natural action in the illumination of experience and the revelation of its liberating secrets.

PRACTICE SESSION
GRACE
· · ·

It's time to explore your relationship to grace experientially through the practice of two repeating questions. Each person will answer each of the following two questions for fifteen minutes. If you are on your own, you can write out your answers to each question for fifteen minutes. (See the "Ownership of Experience" practice in chapter 1 for more details.)

Tell me a position you have about grace.

See what comes up spontaneously when you consider your attitudes, beliefs, and ideas about grace. You may see that there's a connection between this and the ideas you have around basic trust and whether or not you have the sense of there being an optimizing force in life. It's also an opportunity to look at how you see the role of grace on your spiritual path—the blessings of spiritual energy that bring about true transformation.

Tell me a way you have experienced grace.

It could be specific examples of when you've had the experience of something opening up unexpectedly, something being given to you by life that felt like a gift. And remember, this may include things that were only later seen to be blessings in disguise. It could also be a more general sense of how you've felt the action of grace in your soul's journey or your experience of your process not being something that you can make happen yourself.

. . . . .

Questions and Comments

Student: I'm seeing that grace lives in the heart of the creative process, where there's an efforting, work, then an impasse, and then not knowing and giving up, and then something more. More understanding, more comes in and there's a completion, or a sense of completion. And that the inquiring process is the same. Grace enters through understanding.

A. H. Almaas: The whole of inquiry is based on the presence of baraka. Without it, you just find details about your mind and nothing will happen. The fact that inquiry liberates indicates that some other force begins to function. By inquiring, we're opening ourselves to that force to function. Which is the same thing as you said, that creative process. Inquiry basically is a creative process. It's the creativity of our soul. Or more exactly, the creativity of our true nature expressing itself through the individual consciousness.

S: What is grace?

AH: It's everything that I've been talking about. In the traditions, they say there are two kinds of grace: specific grace and general grace. That was the view of Ibn Arabi, the greatest sheikh of the Sufis. Specific grace is when out of nowhere something happens that brings you freedom and release, good fortune, and brings abundance in your life without you knowing why. You know it's just like that, unasked for. You might feel undeserving, because you didn't do anything. That's called specific grace. That's when you feel showered with grace. Just like my experience with the accident. I came close to death. I mean I could have said, "Looks good over there, in that luminous darkness of stillness. I might as well go there." That would have been grace too, but the grace became a grace in life. Not only for myself but for the whole teaching. That was really the beginning of the teaching. So I say, all this is a gift.

This is specific grace, and that's what most people think grace is. When most people talk about blessing and grace, they think of it that way. Something specific happens, in unusual circumstances, like when you're having a hard time and things are going terribly, and suddenly you see an image of the Virgin Mary, out of nowhere. People call that grace.

And there's also general grace. General grace is the recognition of grace from the boundless dimension. When you're in the boundless dimension, you recognize that everything is grace. The very existence of everything is nothing but love, and it is the love and grace of the absolute, the source that brings everything into existence. It's the same grace we see in specific grace, but there we see it as a little window opening up. With general grace we see that everything is grace. This concept of general grace is difficult for most people to understand, because most people don't see things from that perspective. Most people are living in a limited world. Once in a while, a window opens and they feel showered, or melted, or brought to their knees in gratitude. They feel a sense of grace.

However, there are three kinds of grace in the Diamond Approach. I think some traditions probably include the third kind, but I've never read about it. So the first is specific grace, which happens with certain experiences, and the second is general grace, which is the recognition that the unfoldment of every-thing is the compassion and love of true nature. We could call the third grace the grace of the path, or intermediate grace. It's an earned grace, in the sense that as you work on yourself, as you put in your effort, true nature responds with grace. You can see this earned grace in the sense that as you inquire, your inquiry is then completed by the arising of the qualities of being, of true nature, which is the grace that allows the path to happen and the unfold-ment to continue. It is the action of the optimizing force. What is that? It's the fact that there is an action of grace that works like a force coming through us and on us to develop and deepen our experience. And it is really this intermediate grace, the grace of the path, that I've been focusing on in this chapter. That's what I'm trying to point to for us to see that without that, nothing really would happen. Or at least, not much would happen.

And then there is also that concept of grace as baraka, which as I said is a larger concept of specific grace, with the recognition that anything good that happens in your life is a blessing. If you win the lottery, that's a blessing. If your marriage is successful, that's a blessing. And if your meditation takes you to a deep place, that's a blessing. With the term "baraka" I am enlarging the con-cept of specific grace to include good fortune and opportunities in life. So it is not only spiritual happenings.

S: And what was the second kind of grace?

AH: That's general grace, as seen from a boundless dimension such as Divine Love. Now, the third grace, the grace of the path, if you really understand that, you get to see more about how grace works. Because on the path, even the difficulties turn out to be windows or opportunities. Understanding that is why, when I read or listen to people talking about ways of working with trauma or abuse, I often feel there's something missing there. The element of grace is not recognized completely. In that motorcycle experience of mine, for instance, leaving the body could be seen as a dissociation that is typical of trauma. And it was complete dissociation—I was gone. And people often talk about the dissociative disorders that can happen as a result of that. But that dissociation wasn't a bad thing for me. It was not simply a defensive or protective maneuver.

S: Is dissociation always positive in trauma?

AH: Well, I'm not saying that most traumatized people dissociate in this way. Dissociation *is* usually a protective act—it's a way of managing difficult situations. But I'm saying that because of that accident, and also from working with various people with similar experiences, I recognize that in working with dissociation, it's not enough to just get the person to feel and remember their experience, which is the usual therapeutic approach of getting the person to confront the situation. We need to also consider the role of grace in getting over trauma.

Because of my experience of that trauma, when I was first exploring the question of basic trust and living daylight, I realized that I'd already been feeling basic trust without even naming it. It was something that was very much present throughout my process, and then when it came to me working with people, one of the questions that arose for me was what makes some people seem to move smoothly on our path, while others seem to get stuck a lot of the time. And I recognized that one important factor was that it has to do with basic trust. It had always been there for me unconsciously—it was an example of an unthought known. But when I was seeing it in relation to the people I was working with, I started to see that the whole issue of basic trust was related to the experience of the holding environment in early childhood. And what I saw was that as the people I worked with explored this issue of basic trust, and I felt the guidance of it in myself, a channel opened up—the channel of living daylight or divine love. Each of the qualities can open up as a channel when the teacher becomes an embodiment of that quality for the people they are working with.

S: As you've described your experience, of coming out into the street, I don't see any functioning of intention in that. So I'm wondering . . .

AH: No, I had no intention. That's what I'm saying.

S: Right. So I'm wondering if there's a place for intention in relation to grace.

AH: The way I'm looking at it, that experience, that was specific grace. I wasn't intending anything. I was just trying to get home because I needed to go to sleep. I was a little bit tipsy after a couple of glasses of wine and that's all that was happening. So what occurred there is an example of specific grace. It's in the process of following the path where intention arises. That's what I've talked about, the mutual interaction of the work of spiritual practice and grace.

S: What became very clear to me in the first exercise was how my relationship with grace is totally imbedded in object relations. It seems to be something about my relationship to father. There was a whole sense that on an emotional level, the ideal image is that there'd be a big father standing behind me who would catch me if I fell, who would guide me.

AH: Right.

S: And then there was all this complex of beliefs telling me that there never would be a father there for me. Part of that was a belief that I wasn't good enough, and I wasn't really loved, and I wasn't really held. But there was also some idea connected to it that there wasn't any real grace. That grace was totally random; it wasn't related to anything you did or who you were. It was just totally arbitrary and therefore if it ever came, you couldn't depend on it because it would just disappear, it wouldn't have anything to do with me. So I could see there were all these different ideas or attitudes in me because of being imbedded in this object relation, and one of the central ones was the sense of being isolated, being alone, that there wasn't some figure there, some source there for me.

AH: Yes, that makes sense, because really the openness to grace has a lot to do with basic trust, as we have discussed. Basic trust is not a thought, it's not a belief, it's not any particular state. It's something that is preverbal. It's just trust that you're going to be taken care of, that things will work out, and the best is going to happen. And that basic trust obviously has to do with the early holding environment, of both parents and the general situation. So grace is very much related to living daylight, which as we've seen is an expression of divine love. And that's what most people think of as grace or as blessing.

And your talking about your father also reminds me of the first time I recognized directly that in some sense this quality of divine love also has to do with father. The relationship with father is very important to it. What I'm remembering was one of those unasked-for experiences. I think I was finishing dinner, and I was just getting up, and I have this memory: I just see my father going to his bedroom. That's all. He's just opening the door and going in. And suddenly I'm in a completely different place. What's totally there is both divine love and basic trust. I go for a walk and I realize I'm not walking. The body is walking, and I am holding the body, surrounding the body from everywhere there is complete lightness, with no restriction of any sort. That was divine love.

So what happened? I mean I wasn't particularly looking for anything. And I realized that this little memory reminded me of a certain ambiance that was in the house at certain times. I think it was the fact that my father was there, that's all. And that meant everybody was fine, nothing was going wrong. That created a certain ambiance of basic trust, some kind of holding, and that experience is really what led me, by going through it more, to recognize that for a long time I wasn't allowing myself to see my father's love. That my father did love me, but for some reason I didn't see it because he did all kinds of other things. But recognizing my father's love is really what connected me to that, to divine love and living daylight. Because if my father wasn't loving, then the whole world is in some sense going to be hostile.

So definitely to have a good childhood is also grace. For people who are lucky enough to have had a good childhood, where there was love and care and security, that will definitely make their life a positive one. But the situation doesn't stop there because even the most difficult childhood could have its grace too. Some people who made great discoveries and learned a lot and matured a lot had difficult childhoods. And sometimes it was because they had difficult childhoods. That can happen. But generally speaking, having a positive childhood means grace, means more blessing. Blessing is something mysterious, as you see, something magical;

you cannot order it that way. It is not possible to give it a precise order or logic. And the fact that you find a teaching, that by itself is a great opportunity, an example of grace.

So, I began this book by saying that we were going on a journey beyond the dimension of the individual soul, exploring the boundless dimensions. We've ended by looking at the role our effort and practices play in that journey and contrasting that with the blessing, grace, or baraka that is necessary for the truth of those dimensions to be revealed to us and for us to be able to embody that truth in our lives. We need to always remember that without grace, the work won't happen, our life won't go right. If we really understand the teaching and the path, it's possible to be aware of and experience baraka, blessing, or grace always in our lives, in all situations—physically, psychologically, and spiritually. But for that to happen, we really need to be open to it. We need to acknowledge and admit that it is there. If we are not open to this truth—that it is functioning in our life—it tends not to function much. So of course, if we have resistance to it, if we oppose it, if we are closed to it, we will tend not to experience it. This is why the question of allowing, openness, and not knowing is fundamental to this path. But all this allowing, this openness, this not knowing is based on the trust, the faith, that *something* will do it and that everything's going to work out. That aids, and is aided by, our relaxing, by us letting everything be. So although as we've seen, the journey can ultimately end in the realization that we *are* divine love, along the way there is a need to constantly remember that I'm not the one who's doing it—it's always a gift. It's always a blessing and it's always unexpected.

INDEX

Beloved, the, xix, 147, 150, 201
blessings, 3–4, 56, 189–90,
196–97. *See also* grace
body, physical
attachment to, 39–40
birth and death of, 71–72
death and, 61, 62, 134–35
disidentification with, 70
dissociation with, 72–73
enlightenment within, 85–86
essence and, 78, 79
essential aspects and, 48
identification with, 60–63, 66,
68–69, 70, 76, 97–99
as presence, 74
soul and, 41–42, 75, 112
body image, 59–60
body of light, 64–65, 76, 120
boundless dimensions, 1–2, 43,
44, 51, 77, 120
author's experience of, 143–44
barriers to understanding, 2–3
being in, 139–41
Diamond Approach under-
standing of, 42–43
diamond issues in, 59
essential aspects and, 48
existence and, 67
father in, 185
as formless dimensions, 6–7
grace from, 207, 208, 213
memory of, 24–25
need for, 48
perspective of, 79

physical pain and, 40
See also Absolute dimension;
Divine Love dimension;
Supreme dimension
boundlessness, 20, 83, 178
of being, 106–7
experiencing, 9, 10, 63, 100,
144, 150–51
and personal, transitions
between, 145, 146, 150
realizing, levels of, 136–37
Brahman, 121, 140
Buddha, 144, 155
buddha nature, 151
buddhas, 29
Buddhist tradition, 32, 33, 144,
151, 204

Christ consciousness, xii
Christ love, 22
Christian tradition, 32, 144, 185,
204
compassion, 3, 49, 74, 133
as essential aspect, 42, 47
grace and, 203, 208
as green essence, 77
for oneself, 159
pain and, 80
confidence, 197, 200, 204
consciousness, xiii, 134
contraction in, 158, 160
divine love and, 4, 119
equilibrium in, 45–46
without experiencer, 9–10, 14